Contents

For Tim, James and Peter

Going for gold

Eric Liddell

He looked a very ordinary little boy. 'A bit weedy,' thought his new schoolmaster. 'Just as well he has an older brother to stick up for him.' Who could have guessed that the shy six-year-old would one day win an Olympic gold medal, or that many years later he would be the subject of an award winning film?

Eric Liddell looked round his new surroundings. 'I wish I could go back to China with dad and mum,' he thought. He remembered the good times he had had with Rob and Jenny and their Chinese friends racing round the mission compound. He thought of their kind nanny who called him 'Yellee' because she couldn't say his name properly. But it was no use. He was here, at boarding school in London. He'd have to make the best of it.

It wasn't so bad after all. Eric didn't really enjoy sitting behind a desk, but he *did* enjoy games. He could run fast and that was a help on the rugby field. His brother Rob was good at games, too. By the time Eric was sixteen and Rob seventeen they were taking it in turns to win the events at sports day.

In 1920 Eric left school and began to study for a science degree at Edinburgh University. One day a friend called to see him. 'You know the athletic sports will be on in six weeks' time. Didn't you do some running at school? You must enter.'

Eric shook his head. 'Sorry, I'm too busy. I've got a lot of work to do.' But it wasn't so easy to bury his head in his books all the time. Eric loved running and so he started to train for the sports.

Innes Stuart was expected to win the 100 yards. 'He'll be a Scottish champion one day,' people thought. But they were in for a shock. The first year student, Liddell, beat Stuart in the final! The University was buzzing with the news. Stuart just managed to beat Eric in the 200 yards, but that was the last race Eric ever lost in Scotland.

Eric was a great sport but he certainly didn't like to be beaten. His unusual running style would make him the despair of an athletics coach today. As he approached the tape, he would throw his head back so he couldn't see where he was going and he'd hit out with his fists. Amazingly he nearly always won.

'Will you come?' Eric was faced with an important question. The man wasn't asking him to take part in an athletics match, but a Christian meeting. Most people in Scotland knew Eric's name. He was a famous athlete. But not many people knew about his Christian faith. That was something he'd kept pretty much to himself. But now he knew that had got to change. He agreed to speak at the meeting.

Eric looked at the men in front of him. Could he hold their attention? He began to speak in his rather flat, quiet voice. He told the men about the difference Jesus made to his life. They didn't shuffle in their seats. They didn't look bored. They wanted to hear what he had to say. 'He's not just talk. He really means it,' they thought. 'Maybe it would work for us, too.'

The Olympic Games, to be held in Paris in 1924, were coming nearer. Who would be selected to represent Great Britain? Eric was a famous athlete in Scotland, but he still had to show his form south of the border. He entered for the AAAs championship in London and won the 100 yards in record breaking time. The next week he won the 100 yards again at another big athletics meeting. That was it. There was no doubt. Eric Liddell would represent Great Britain in the 100 metres race at the Paris Olympics. Or so everyone thought.

Eric looked glumly at the paper in front of him. It was the timetable for the Olympic Games. The heats for the 100 metres were to be on a Sunday. Eric believed that Sunday was God's special day. He had never raced on a Sunday before and he wasn't going to start now.

'Liddell won't race on a Sunday!' The British Olympic official exploded. 'He's throwing away a gold medal!'

Eric was unhappy. He loved his country. It would be wonderful to win a gold medal for Scotland, but he had to stick to his principles and he wouldn't change his mind.

The athletics authorities didn't want to lose Eric from the team altogether. They asked him to enter the 200 and 400 metre races. Eric was good at 400 metres, but was he good enough? He arrived in Paris with only an outside chance against the other competitors, many of whom had made better times than he had.

The Sunday heats for the 100 metres came and went. Eric was not in the stadium. Instead, he was preaching at a church too far away to hear the cheering as Harold Abrahams won his heat for Great Britain. The next day, Abrahams went on to win the 100 metres. So Britain had the gold after all. Eric was glad. But did he feel just a twinge of regret that it was Abrahams and not he who was standing on the rostrum to receive the gold medal?

Three days later, Eric raced in his heat for the 400 metres. He qualified for the next round but his time of 50.2 seconds was not impressive. Could he do better in the quarter final? '49.0 seconds. My best time ever!' Eric smiled as he heard the result. But he knew that even that would not be good enough in the final. Tomorrow it would be decided. Tomorrow he would run the race of his life.

Eric won his semi-final race in 48.2 seconds. Would he be able to beat the American runner, Fitch, who had just set a new Olympic record in the other semi-final? The six finalists arrived on the track, but before they could come under starters orders they were startled by the strident blare of the bagpipes. Some Scottish soldiers were in the stadium and no one could stop them as they piped out their special encouragement for Eric Liddell. Then it was back to business.

'Crack!' went the starting pistol. Eric was in the outside lane. He set off at an amazing speed. The crowd gasped as he rounded the bend at the half way point, two metres ahead of his rivals. 'He'll never keep it up,' some thought. Fitch was straining to close on him. But then, from somewhere, Eric found extra power. He began to widen the gap until he lunged across the finishing tape five metres ahead of Fitch. The time, 47.6 seconds, was a new world record. The crowd went wild. All around the stadium Union Jacks were waving. He'd done it! Olympic gold for Scotland. No one could call him unpatriotic now.

Six days later, the students of Edinburgh University were to receive their degrees. When it came to Eric's turn, everyone stood up and cheered him. The University principal placed an olive wreath, like those given to the winners of the Olympic Games in Ancient Greece, on Eric's head. Still wearing the wreath, Eric was carried by students from the hall along the streets of Edinburgh.

The next day, there was a dinner given in Eric's honour. 'I wish they would get it over with,' he thought, as he listened to the speeches praising his Olympic victory. He didn't like to be the centre of that sort of attention. He stood up to reply to the speeches. Everyone was listening. 'I won't be making running my career,' he told them. 'I'm going to China. I'm going to be a missionary.'

His news may have come as a shock to some of the people listening, but for Eric it was no sudden decision. He wanted to tell others about Jesus and he knew that in China there were many people waiting to hear. Now that he had a degree he would be able to get a job as a teacher in China. But first he must spend a year at college learning more from the Bible. What a year! Eric studied hard, but in the evenings and at weekends he was off to speak at meetings or to train or race. It was soon over. Eric packed his bags and got ready to leave for China.

'What's happening?' 'Look at the crowds!' 'The students must be up to something!' They were! The people of Edinburgh crowded the pavements to watch as Eric was taken in a carriage, pulled by students, to the station. On the station platform people were waving, cheering and singing hymns. Eric loved it. He had some wonderful memories to take with him to China.

Eric put down the report he had been reading and stared out of the train window. He had plenty of time to read and think on his long journey across Western Europe, Poland and Russia. The train crossed the vast plains of Siberia. Soon he would be heading south into China, on the last stage of his journey to Tient-sin. The reports did not make cheerful reading. Many people in China were fighting each other. There had been floods and food was short.

A full scale war between the Nationalist Party and the Communist Party might break out at any time. The Chinese wanted to be in charge of their own country. They didn't like the foreign business men who were making a lot of money from the tea and silk and cotton produced in China. Some people didn't like the missionaries, either. 'The Communist Party has called a strike.' The message went round. Workers stayed away from their factories. Students stayed away from their colleges. Many stayed away from the school where Eric was due to start teaching.

'That's how it is.' The teachers looked a bit embarrassed as they broke the news to Eric. He had come a long way to start his first job and now they had to tell him that there might not be a job to start. 'We'll open the school as usual after the summer holidays and see

matters worse, soldiers were fighting all around them. The Chinese Nationalists and the Communists had been so busy fighting each other that they had failed to stop the invasion by Japanese soldiers. Now the Japanese controlled many of the railway lines and big cities. But the countryside around Siaochang was still held by the Chinese. If the Chinese guerilla fighters blew up a train, the Japanese would take it out on the ordinary Chinese peasants. The frightened people of Siaochang knew of only one place they could go for protection and help – to the mission compound. The women and children sheltered in the church during bombing attacks. Eric's brother, Rob, was working as a doctor in the mission hospital. It was always packed out with very sick people.

In spite of the dangers and hardships, Eric enjoyed his work. He loved the people and the people loved him. He travelled to many villages, sometimes walking, sometimes by bike. When a crowd had gathered round, he would talk to them. They could tell that he understood how sad and difficult their lives were. They listened carefully as he talked about Jesus. He stayed in the homes of his Chinese friends. If they went hungry, Eric went hungry, too. The journey back to Tientsin, which was held by the Japanese, was full of dangers.

It was good to get away at last. Eric and Florence were looking forward to their time in Canada and Scotland. But even in Britain they might not be safe from fighting. It was 1939. The world was on the brink of war. When he got to Scotland, Eric volunteered to be an R.A.F. pilot. 'They turned me down,' he told Florence in disgust. 'Said I was too old and offered me a desk job.' Eric wasn't having that. In 1940 the family returned to China.

Back in Siaochang, things were even worse than before. One day a nurse bustled into the operating theatre and discovered a Japanese soldier hitting the doctor with a baton. Soon the missionaries were given their orders. 'You will leave in two weeks' time.' Eric returned to Tientsin. Would the British be put into Japanese camps? It seemed likely. Eric decided that Florence, who was expecting another baby, and the girls, must go back to Canada. 'Be a good girl,' he told Patricia. 'Look after mummy for me, and Heather, and the new baby.' He didn't know that he would never see his third daughter.

At 6am in Weihsien Internment Camp, Eric climbed out of his bunk bed. Quietly he made his way across the dormitory to the little table where he sat to pray and read the Bible. He needed this time. Time to get close to God, to ask for strength for the busy day ahead. His days were very full – fetching water, cleaning, translating for the Japanese, teaching Maths and Science, organising camp sports, mending broken hockey sticks, leading the Christian Fellowship, helping everyone who turned to him, cheering people up with his infectious smile.

It was especially hard for the teenagers to be cooped up in an internment camp. They needed interesting things to do. Eric helped by organising model making, chess and country dancing and by refereeing hockey matches.

There were no matches organised on Sundays. But one Sunday, the teenagers decided to play a match, boys against girls. It ended in a fight. 'They must have a referee in future,' Eric thought. The next Sunday he turned up to do the job. He had given up his chance of an Olympic gold medal in the 100 metres because of his views on keeping Sunday special. But he was willing to break his rule to keep the peace between a crowd of teenagers.

Few people knew about Eric's dreadful headaches, caused by a massive brain tumour. News of his death stunned the whole camp. How would they ever manage without him? Among those who missed him most were the teenagers. But many people treasured their memories of a very special man who loved God and loved people.

The film about Eric Liddell, 'Chariots of Fire', won the 1981 Oscar Award for the Best Picture of the Year.

All your watches are safe

Corrie ten Boom

The summer holidays! 'Wonderful,' thought Corrie. 'I'll be able to go to Amsterdam with Father to collect the time.' Corrie's father was a watchmaker, the best in Holland, some people said. Every Monday he travelled by train from Haarlem to Amsterdam to check his pocket watch against the signal from the naval Observatory at twelve noon. There were no time checks on the radio. The radio had not yet been invented. But with his pocket watch now telling exactly the right time, Father ten Boom could correct the 'astronomical clock' which stood in his shop.

As the train left Haarlem, Corrie peered out of the windows at the fields, canals, windmills and tidy farm houses. Soon they would be in Amsterdam. Before the time check, Father had to visit a wholesaler to buy watches and spare parts. The man who greeted them was a Jew. He had a long, bushy beard. 'Even longer than Father's,' Corrie noticed. It didn't take long for Father to buy the things he needed. Then the two men got down to the business they enjoyed most – discussing the Bible. 'Have you noticed what it says in the book of Isaiah . . .'

'But, of course, my friend . . .'

'Have they forgotten me?' Corrie wondered. She needn't have worried. Before long their bearded friend was hunting in cupboards and handing Corrie a plate of the most delicious sweets and cakes she had ever tasted.

The train journey home was Corrie's special talking time with Father. She knew he was always ready to talk to her. As she grew up they discussed the future. 'Isn't it wonderful that Betsie is graduating from secondary school? I hope she will be able to keep the books for me in the shop.' 'Willem has got his scholarship for university.' Corrie was proud of her younger brother. And as for Corrie? She'd be staying at home to help Aunt Anna with the work in the crowded old house where Corrie, her mother and father, sisters Betsie and Nollie, brother Willem and three aunts all lived.

The years passed by. Corrie was still at home. Her one and only boy-friend had married another girl. Mother and the aunts were dead. Willem and Nollie were married with their own families. Corrie now worked as a watchmaker in Father's shop while Betsie looked after the house. Her life was busy and happy and settled. She was a respectable middle-aged lady. How could she know what adventures and hardships were just around the corner?

It was January 1937. A hundred years since Corrie's grandfather had put up a sign in his window – TEN BOOM — WATCHES. Today was the shop's birthday party. The door bell rang. 'More flowers!' cried Betsie. The shop was beginning to look like a florist's. Then the callers began to arrive, streaming in to shake hands with Father ten Boom, now a wonderful white haired old man. The party went on all day. Tea and cakes were passed round. Children arrived after school. Nollie and her family came. But where was Willem? It was getting dark before he and his family arrived. They were not alone. The buzz of conversation stopped as everyone stared in horror at the man by Willem's side. He was wearing a big, black hat often worn by Jews. His face was horribly burnt. He had escaped from Germany, Willem explained. 'Some teenage boys set fire to his beard.'

Something terrible was happening in Germany, Holland's next door neighbour. Corrie and Betsie tried not to think about it too much, but it was hard to avoid the screams of Adolf Hitler which bellowed at them from the radio set. Then letters from Jewish watch suppliers in Germany were returned 'Address unknown'. What was Hitler doing to the Jews? How long would Holland be safe from this madness?

It was 1939. Two years since the shop's birthday party. Father, Corrie and Betsie sat round the table on which the big radio was kept. England, France and Germany were already at war. Was Holland going to join in? Soon they would know. The Prime Minister's voice came over the radio: 'No war . . . nothing to fear . . . Dutchmen should stay calm . . .'.

But Father knew better. It was wrong to give people false hope.

That night Corrie woke with a start. The sky lit up. Her bed rocked with the explosion. She made her way downstairs, stopping at Father's door. He was still asleep.

'Betsie, Betsie!' The sisters threw their arms around each other. Holland was at war.

Five days later, Holland surrendered. German tanks came rumbling over the border. Haarlem was full of soldiers. Everyone had to produce an identity card on demand. People didn't trust the newspapers any more. They were hungry for news of how the war was going.

'Your turn to listen to the radio tonight, Corrie.' Radios were not allowed. The ten Boom's would be in a lot of trouble if the Nazis discovered the set hidden under the floor board. Corrie turned the volume up just enough to hear the BBC news while Betsie played loudly on the piano. The news was bad. There was no sign of Hitler being defeated yet.

'That must be Betsie in the kitchen.' Corrie climbed out of bed to join her sister. It was the middle of the night but she couldn't sleep. Planes were fighting over Haarlem. They drank tea until the noise stopped. Corrie was about get back into bed when her hand touched something hard and sharp on the pillow. A piece of metal shrapnel! Corrie's heart raced. She knew the shrapnel could have killed her. But God had other plans.

'Did you hear about the synagogue being burnt down?' 'They are refusing to serve Jews in the restaurant.' 'Jews are not even allowed in the library now.' Things were getting worse and worse for the Jewish people. They had to wear a yellow star on their coats so that they would be marked out as second class citizens. Worst of all, many disappeared, herded into the back of trucks, never to be seen again.

One morning Corrie saw four soldiers marching down the street. They stopped outside a shop which sold furs. 'Bang!' the rifle thumped against the door and soon the soldiers were inside. Mr Weil, the Jewish shop owner, came out backwards with a rifle butt in his stomach. He stood, grey faced, on the pavement while the soldiers emptied his shop. But he was not arrested . . . this time. When the soldiers had gone, Corrie guided the stunned old man into her house. 'We must warn your wife not to return from Amsterdam,' she said. 'It's not safe for either of you to be here. My brother, Willem, may know of a place in the country where you can stay.' And so Mr Weil left, escorted into the darkness by Willem's son, Kik.

'What's happened to Mr and Mrs Weil?' Corrie asked Kik next time she saw him. He smiled but didn't answer her. It was best not to ask questions, or to answer them when you were working for the Underground.

The Underground was an illegal group of people working against the Nazis and helping those in danger, like the Jews, to find safe hiding places. It was very dangerous work. Was Corrie willing to get involved? She loved Jesus and Jesus was a Jew. 'Yes,' she decided. She would do what she could to help his people. She didn't have long to wait.

One evening a lady turned up on the doorstep. She was a Jewess, frightened for her life. Before long she was joined in the ten Boom's house by a man and wife who were also escaping from the Nazis. 'They need to go to places in the country. I'll visit Willem and see if he can help,' Corrie decided. But Willem told her it was getting more and more difficult to place people and impossible unless they had ration cards.

Jews were not issued with ration cards. Corrie needed a private source of supply. She thought of a friend who worked in the Food Office. Perhaps he could arrange something? And so it was that a hundred ration cards were delivered each month, hidden under a loose floorboard by a man dressed as a meter reader.

More and more people came for help. 'A Jewish man has died in hiding. How can he be buried without the authorities finding out who he is?' 'Where can a Jewish woman safely have a baby?' Corrie knew lots of people in Haarlem, but whom could she trust? 'I don't know. But God does. I must ask him to show me,' she decided.

It wasn't safe to talk about the Underground work over the phone, so Corrie and her friends worked out a code. They talked about 'watches' instead of 'Jews'. 'A watch needs mending' meant 'a Jewish person needs a hiding place.'

There were always extra people in Corrie's house – Jews or Underground workers. They needed a hiding place in case of a raid by the Gestapo, the Nazi Secret Police.

Corrie, Betsie and Father stared in amazement at the wall in Corrie's bedroom. It looked exactly the same as it had always looked, dirty from coal dust and stained in places. But it was *not* the same. It was a new, false wall and behind it was a secret room. The architect of the secret room, a member of the Underground, looked pleased with his work. This one should fool them.

Corrie crept out of bed, felt her way down the stairs in the darkness and pressed the button underneath the dining room window. 'Buzz..zz.' The alarm sounded through the house. The extra members of the household were out of bed in seconds, grabbing their sheets and turning their mattresses. A warm patch on a mattress was a give-away to the Secret Police. They panted upstairs, dived into Corrie's bedroom at the top of the house, slid back the secret panel and were in the hiding place. 'Practice over!' Corrie greeted them. Everyone breathed sighs of relief. 'Seventy seconds. That's very good. It took four minutes for our first practice.' Then she produced the special treat kept only to sweeten the nerve-wracking practices – a bag of cream puffs!

It was nearly Christmas 1943. The Dutch people were sad and worried. Many would go to church to remember that God had been born as a baby into a hard, cruel world. In Corrie's house they also celebrated the Jewish festival called Hanukkah. The candles flickered and everyone gathered round the piano to sing the beautiful traditional songs.

'Brrr.' The door bell rang. Corrie answered it and came back to the others looking worried. It was their next door neighbour asking them not to sing so loudly. She knew about the Jews in the house. 'If *she* knows, who else does . . .?' Corrie wondered.

On a Saturday morning in January 1944 Corrie had 'flu: aching joints, hot and cold shivers, a splitting headache. Bed was the best place to be. A harsh noise penetrated her dream. She opened her eyes. 'The buzzer!' Her heart thumped as the door opened and a stream of frightened people dived into the secret room behind the false wall of her bedroom. The raid! It was happening. Seconds later, a tall, burly man of the Secret Police barged into the room.

If only it could have been a dream! But the nightmare of that day was all too real. Their house was turned into a trap. Each caller was arrested until at last news of the raid got around and the doorbell stopped ringing. Then Corrie and the thirty four other prisoners were taken to the police station. As for the six people hiding in the secret room? – Corrie couldn't bear to think about them. True, the soldiers hadn't found where the room was – yet. But they were sure it was there and they were keeping a guard on the house. How long would it take to starve the fugitives out of their hiding place?

The army lorry bumped along the road. Corrie put her arm behind Father to prevent his head from hitting the side of the truck. They had been taken from the local police station to the national Gestapo Headquarters. Now where were they going? The lorry stopped to allow huge iron gates to open and then took them inside the prison walls.

Corrie lay down at last on the dirty straw mattress in the cell. The dust made her cough worse. 'How are Father and Betsie?' she wondered. Corrie missed them dreadfully. Worrying about them made her feel worse still. Her four cell mates were unhappy at having a sick person with them and she was unlikely to get better quickly in this place.

Getting along with four people cooped up in a cell was hard. But soon Corrie had to face something even harder – solitary confinement. She had been taken to the hospital to see the doctor. She could be infectious. And so she was alone in a cell, even colder than the last, staring at the four walls. But one good thing had happened during her trip to the hospital. A kind nurse had secretly given her a small newspaper parcel. Inside were some safety pins, soap – and the four gospels. As Corrie began to get better she read more and more. Jesus knew what it was to suffer. He was arrested, beaten, killed. But that wasn't the end of the story. Because of that, we could be God's friends and live with him for ever. Something wonderful and good could come from what seemed like defeat.

'A parcel – for me!' Corrie set to work to undo the string. What riches! All things to make prison life more bearable – a sweater, a towel, vitamin drops, biscuits, a needle and cotton. Corrie took another look at the brown wrapping paper. The writing was slanting up to the postage stamp. 'That's strange. There couldn't be, could there . . . a message underneath the stamp?' She soaked off the stamp and at last made out a coded message in tiny writing. '*All the watches in your cupboard are safe.*' Everyone had escaped from the secret room! Corrie cried with joy and relief.

'Why am I frightened to open it?' Corrie held the letter in her hand. It was the first she had received since being in prison. It contained sad news. Father was dead. He had lived only ten days after his arrest.

Corrie hurried along the corridor after the German officer. She must be there for the reading of her father's will. She stepped inside the office. There they were! Willem, Nollie and Betsie. They hugged and talked for a few precious minutes and Nollie gave Corrie a present. Quickly she opened it while the German officer was not looking. 'A Bible!' It fitted into a little bag with a long string so she could wear it round her neck hidden underneath her clothes.

'Where are we going?' Corrie wondered sometime later as she stood in the station yard with hundreds of other prisoners. 'Why have the Germans evacuated the prison? Perhaps the allied troops have already landed in Holland?' Then in the distance she spotted Betsie. Could she get to her? 'Please, Lord, don't let the trains come until it gets dark.' Everyone was pressing forwards to climb aboard. Corrie made her way sideways until at last she seized Betsie's hand. They got on the train. Wherever they were going, they were going together.

So this was a concentration camp. Every morning the prisoners had to stand to attention for the long roll call. There was cruel punishment for those who didn't toe the line. Everyone was expected to work for eleven hours a day. Corrie's job was assembling radios for fighter planes. Betsie spent the day sewing prison clothes – and secretly telling other women about God's love for them.

The German guards were getting more and more tense. The war was not going their way. 'How long will it be before we are freed?' the prisoners wondered. 'Will our soldiers come soon?'

They didn't come soon enough. Once again Corrie, Betsie and the other prisoners were moved on. This time into Germany.

After a nightmare journey herded into cattle trucks they reached their destination – Ravensbruck, an even worse camp than the one they had left. The camp was in a valley, surrounded by a huge wall topped with electrified wire. Their first night was spent on the cinder covered ground, with only a blanket between them and the torrential rain. A second night out in the open followed and then they were officially 'admitted'.

Corrie felt the Bible in its pouch bumping against her back. 'How are we going to get it past the inspection?' she wondered. 'We need it so badly.' In the shower room were some old benches. Corrie hid the Bible behind them. After her shower, she put on one of the prison dresses and hung the Bible pouch back round her neck. They lined up for inspection. The guards searched the woman in front of Corrie. They searched Betsie, who was behind her in the line. But no one touched Corrie or spotted the Bible.

'Give thanks in all circumstances.' Corrie read the words from the Bible. But what could she thank God for here – in this overcrowded, dirty, smelly, flea-ridden dormitory? For letting her be there with Betsie, for the other women who would hear God speaking through the Bible, for the fleas . . . 'I can't thank God for the fleas!' But Betsie insisted. Only later did they learn that it was because of the fleas that the guards kept away from their dormitory.

Morning roll call was at 4.40am. Then the prisoners had to work hard all day with only a ladle of soup and one potato to eat at lunch-time. Everyone grew desperately thin. Corrie could see Betsie getting weaker and weaker. Their life was very, very hard.

But in the evenings they met with a growing number of other prisoners to worship God. They knew his love in a way they had never dreamt possible.

Betsie died that winter. Corrie's heart ached for the

sister she had loved so dearly. But she knew that Betsie was free now – free from the horrors of Ravensbruck, free from pain and hunger and with Jesus.

'Betsie was sure we'd *both* be out of Ravensbruck by the new year,' Corrie remembered, 'and she was right.' Amazingly Corrie had been released. No explanation was given. But here she was at the railway station waiting to go home to Holland. It wasn't until many years later that she learnt that she had been freed by mistake! That's what they told her – but Corrie knew that *God* doesn't make mistakes.

After the war, Corrie ran a home for people who were still suffering mentally or physically because of what they had been through. She travelled to over sixty countries telling of how God could work even in a place like Ravensbruck. She died in 1983 – on her ninety-first birthday. The film about Corrie's life is called *The Hiding Place*.

Surgeon on top of the world

Ruth Watson

There was a rustling in the trees. On the floor of the forest, branches snapped beneath heavy feet. A man walking home along the path from the rice fields turned and stopped in his tracks. Then, his heart racing, he ran and ran. But not fast enough. The great black Himalayan bear grabbed him from behind and tore his face with its claws.

The night was cold. Inside their smoke-filled room, the Nepali family huddled round the fire. When they lay down on the hard floor to sleep they put the children nearest to the glowing embers. The little girl's screams awoke them all. 'She must have rolled over in her sleep,' someone said. Now they looked with horror at her hideous burns.

Who could they turn to? And who could help the man mauled by the bear? There was no hospital, no doctor, not even a qualified nurse. The people in the beautiful Kingdom of Nepal, high up in the Himalayas, were almost completely cut off from the outside world.

But 8000 miles away, God had been working in the life of a young English girl. He was preparing her for a special job, to show the love of Jesus to the people of

Nepal by helping to mend their broken bodies.

Ruth Watson grew up in Coventry, a big industrial city in the Midlands. She lived there with her mum and dad, older brothers John and Colin, and her younger sister Jill. Her dad was a clever engineer who worked on ways to make better, more efficient cars. Before they went to bed, Ruth and the others would look into his study to say goodnight. Sometimes they found him still there, hard at work, the next morning! Ruth was like her dad, clever and full of energy and ideas. She hated to sit still and do nothing.

One day, there was bad news on the radio. Mum and Dad looked worried. The Second World War was starting. 'It isn't safe for the children to be in Coventry,' said Dad. 'There are so many factories. It's bound to be a target for the bombers.' The boys were already at boarding school, and Dad said Jill must go too. But Ruth stayed on at the King's High School in Warwick. Instead of catching a bus for the ten-mile journey each day, she went to live with a school friend in Warwick, a much safer place than Coventry.

'It's for me!' Ruth's heart thumped as she opened the official looking envelope. Inside was a letter from Birmingham University Medical School. 'They have accepted my application! I'm going to be a doctor.' The war was coming to an end. Ruth was in her last year at school. She was tired of the air raid sirens, the bombs, the hurting and killing. She wanted to make the world a better place.

Ruth was looking forward to the summer holidays, too. She had agreed to go with a friend to a camp organised by a Christian group called the Girls' Crusader Union. 'I won't bother to listen to the Christian talks,' she thought. 'But I can enjoy the rest of the camp. It looks as though they have some good things planned.'

But it wasn't so easy to ignore the talks. Ruth became ill at camp and, staying in bed, she had plenty of time to think over what the leaders had been saying. 'Jesus is the Son of God. He died for me. He wants to be my Saviour. I have to choose whether I'm going to follow him and let him be in charge of my life, or not.' The thoughts wouldn't go away. At last Ruth made up her mind. 'I'm yours, Lord Jesus. I give my life to you – all of it.' It was the most important decision she ever made.

'Oh, the smell! Am I going to be sick?' Ruth and the other new medical students had just begun their first practical anatomy lesson. Ruth forced herself to look at the dead body in front of her. It was preserved in formalin, a strong-smelling liquid. But gradually her queasy feelings disappeared as she learned to identify the different veins and arteries, bones and muscles. Yes, medicine was fascinating. In spite of the exams and hard work, Ruth loved her time as a medical student. But she still had decisions to take.

There are many different branches of medicine which a newly qualified doctor may follow. He can become a family doctor, a surgeon, a specialist in children's illnesses or X-Rays or many other things. Ruth was good at helping with operations.

'Maybe one day I'll be a really good surgeon,' she hoped. But soon after she had given her life to Jesus, she had another thought. 'Perhaps God wants me to be a missionary doctor.' She tried to put the idea out of her mind. 'Missionaries are old-fashioned people who carry big Bibles. I don't want to be like that!' Then she had a surprise. The results of the latest exam in Surgery were on the notice board. 'I've failed.' Ruth looked crestfallen.

'It's only by one mark,' someone reassured her. 'You probably won't have to re-sit.' But Ruth felt her result was a message from God. 'He wants me to be a missionary doctor, not a top class surgeon.' She didn't know at the time that God had plans for her to be *both*!

'I haven't paid all this money for your education so you can waste your life in some far-away place.' Ruth's father was not pleased about her plans to become a missionary. Neither was her mother. 'What opportunity will you have to get married if you go abroad? I was so looking forward to having grandchildren!' Ruth hadn't expected this. She found it so hard to explain. But she was sure that this was what God wanted. And her parents knew they must let her decide for herself.

Before long, Ruth would have to make another decision. She knew that God wanted her to go to another country to show his love to people by helping to mend their bodies, but which country? The world is a big place.

Since she was a young girl, Ruth had loved mountains. She remembered the wonderful time she had had when Dad took the family for winter sports holidays. The bright sun on the snow, the air rushing past her face as her skis swished down the mountain slope. How could she ever forget it? And now she remembered that the highest mountain in the world, Mount Everest, is on the border between Tibet and Nepal.

'Nepal.' It was only a suggestion someone had made. But the more she thought about it, the more certain Ruth became that God wanted her in Nepal, but not for a winter sports holiday! She finished her training, worked as a junior hospital doctor, spent a year at a missionary training college, packed her bags, said her goodbyes (how hard *that* was) and she was off.

If you travelled to Nepal today, you could get there by air in fifteen hours. But Ruth's journey in 1952 was not so straightforward. Not that she minded. 'This sunshine is marvellous', Ruth thought as the boat made its way across the Mediterranean. 'I'm so looking forward to seeing the Pyramids when we get to Egypt.' There were fascinating things to see and there was plenty of time to relax as the voyage continued through the Red Sea and across the Indian Ocean.

India came as quite a shock – so many people, so much noise! With a loud whistle, the train shuddered out of the station. Ruth gaped at the men clinging to the outside of the train. Would they fall off? And what about those sitting on the roof? It was a long, hot journey – fifteen hundred miles from the port of Bombay to the border with Nepal. Ruth longed for a cool drink. But she had to make do with hot sweet tea. At least *that* water had been boiled.

Here they were. Together at last. A small group of missionaries about to enter the Kingdom of Nepal. Ruth got ready for bed. But something was bothering her. 'I haven't cleaned my teeth. The bathroom is down those awful stairs and it's so dark.' Ruth shuddered. She was cross with herself. 'I'm a missionary. I'm not supposed to be afraid!' But she *was* afraid. She didn't clean her teeth that night or ever again before she went to bed!

An army lorry pulled up and two soldiers jumped down. They had come from the British Army Recruiting Centre for the Gurkha Brigade based over the border in Nepal and were going to take Ruth and the others on the next stage of their journey to Pokhara in Nepal. 'Hurry up with those bedding rolls. You don't really need a badminton racquet, do you? There's room for you to squeeze in here.' Somehow the truck was loaded and they were off, bumping their way into Nepal.

It was time for lunch and also time to say goodbye to the helpful soldiers. They were at the end of the road. For the next eight days they would be walking along mountain paths, exhilarated by wonderful views of the snow-covered Himalayas.

Ruth's stomach turned over. Ahead of them was a fast flowing river running through a deep gorge. The only way to cross it was by a suspension bridge which swayed from side to side. Ruth took a deep breath and stepped onto the bridge. God hadn't promised her an easy life, after all.

They were over the bridge and climbing up the next hill when they saw a collection of small mud huts. This was where people with the disease leprosy had to live. They were banished from their villages, had no medicine and were not fed properly. Soldiers were on duty to stop them running away. Ruth's heart went out to them.

'Thank you, Lord, for keeping us safe.' It was the last night of their trek. A cold wind blew from the snow-covered hills. Ruth was glad to be in her warm sleeping bag. Tomorrow they would be in Pokhara – Ruth's home for the next twenty-four years.

It wasn't much of a hospital, but they had to start somewhere. Ruth and the other missionaries worked hard to build their first huts. The walls were made from bamboo and the roots were thatched. Two of the huts were for eating and sleeping in. The third hut was a dispensary where sick people came for medicine and treatment. They built the huts on land belonging to Buddhi Sagar, a Nepali man who had become a Christian in India. More and more people began to join the church which met in Buddhi's house. God's family in Nepal was growing.

'Crack, crack, bang!' People stopped to listen. it must be gunshots. Some men were fighting against the king's soldiers. A few days later, Ruth's eyes widened as she saw a man being carried to the dispensary. He was in bad shape. The smell told her that he already had gangrene in his wounded leg.

'If we don't amputate his leg, he's bound to die,' she said. A small thatched hut is not an ideal operating theatre and Ruth was not a trained surgeon. But she was not put off. 'We've got to help him,' she decided. 'I'm sure there are some surgical instruments in one of these packing cases. If we push the cases together they will do as an operating table.' Amputating a leg is a difficult operation and the medical textbook didn't seem to give many details. 'Please help us, Father God,' Ruth and the others prayed. Then the patient was given chloroform anaesthetic and the operation began.

As the days passed, Ruth watched the man's progress with increasing pleasure. 'He's pulling through. He'll soon be able to go home,' she thought. 'Thank you, Lord.'

News of the mission hospital began to spread. More and more people came for help. 'We must have better buildings,' everyone agreed. They were able to rent a large, flat site. Sturdy new huts were made from aluminium sheets bolted onto steel frames. 'They will be hot in summer and cold in winter,' Ruth knew, 'but at least they will keep out the rain and hail.' The aluminium sheets shone in the sunlight. Local people laughed and dogs barked when they saw themselves in the 'mirror'. The new hospital soon had a name – 'The Shining Hospital'.

Ruth was given a new name, too. In Nepal, the eldest girl in a family is called 'Tuli' and the youngest is called 'Kanchi'. So Pat, an older missionary doctor, was called 'Tuli Doctor' and Ruth was called 'Kanchi Doctor'.

One day, a girl called Maya came to the Shining Hospital. She had chest pains. 'Perhaps the doctors there will be able to make me better,' she thought. But the pains didn't go away. Then she met Hannah, an old lady who loved Jesus. Hannah told Maya that Jesus could make her better if she believed in him. 'I had better find out more,' Maya decided. So she started to read the New Testament. At last she made up her mind. 'Yes,' she thought, 'I'm going to follow Jesus.' She stopped worshipping Hindu gods. Before long the pains in her chest disappeared. 'I must tell the people in my village,' she thought. And soon there was a group of them who believed in Jesus. When Maya met Ruth walking along the road she stopped to tell her the good news. Ruth was thrilled. She invited Maya to come and see her and soon the two of them were the best of friends.

It was good to be in Nepal. It was good to be able to treat so many patients. It was good to be in the place where God had put her. But it wasn't easy. Ruth always wanted to do the best for her patients. But there were not always enough medical supplies to go round. Water had to be boiled before it was safe to drink. Often there was no meat or cheese or eggs to eat. Worse than that, she couldn't always get on with the other missionaries. 'It shouldn't be like this. God wants us to love each other!' Ruth could feel her stomach churning up. In fact her insides never seemed to be right these days. Then there were her asthma attacks. It was frightening not to be able to get your breath. Secretly, Ruth knew that she was ill because she was cross inside and she couldn't tell anyone how she was feeling.

But Ruth couldn't keep her feelings bottled up for ever. Just before she was due to return to England for her first holiday she told one of the older missionaries how unhappy she was. Now it was out in the open. She felt better. But oh, so very tired.

It was wonderful to be able to relax after all the strain and hard work. Ruth lay back in her deck-chair and looked at the calm, blue sea. She was heading home. She could hardly wait to see Mum and Dad and Jill and her friends. 'What a story I've got to tell them! It's been hard. But God has been good.'

A year in England. It sounded a long time, but there was plenty to do. Ruth had to give talks and show slides about her work in Nepal. She also wanted to watch other surgeons at work so that she could learn to do other operations. Ruth remembered the Nepali people she had seen suffering from burns – like the little girl who rolled over into the fire. 'I must learn as much as I can about plastic surgery,' she resolved.

Back in Nepal, Ruth had plenty of opportunity to use her new skills. The Shining Hospital had a shining reputation. Many people with appalling injuries came for help. The operating theatre was far from perfect. Sometimes the lights would go out in the middle of an operation. But Ruth achieved a very high success rate. She worked so fast that germs didn't have time to infect the wounds!

Ruth became the top-class surgeon she had wanted to be since her days as a medical student. Some of her greatest successes were the skin grafts she gave to patients with bad burns. The results were as good as those achieved in any hospital in our country.

Ever since she had first seen people with leprosy, Ruth had wanted to be able to help those suffering from that dreaded disease. A new hospital was opened to treat leprosy patients. The leprosy bacteria could be killed with modern drugs. But the patients were often left badly deformed, without toes, fingers or a nose. I'll ask Dad if he can invent something to help, Ruth thought. Sure enough, her father came up with several good ideas. One was a muscle stimulator run from a battery. It could help to prevent the muscles in a damaged foot from wasting away.

Was it really twenty-four years since she had first come to Pokhara? Ruth was the senior missionary at the hospital. She was as busy as ever. Could that be why she was having such bad headaches? This one was dreadful. 'I must sit down!' Ruth groped for a chair.

'Doctor . . .' One of the nurses bustled into the room. She was alarmed to see Ruth looking so ill. But Ruth wasn't going to be beaten by a headache.

A few days later, she had just finished her round of the hospital wards when she stopped in her tracks. 'What's happening? I can't see properly. I can't find my way out of here.'

Another doctor came to examine Ruth. They both knew what the trouble might be. 'A brain tumour.' Ruth cried as she spoke the words. How could she say goodbye to Pokhara and to the people she loved so much? The next day she boarded the plane for Kathmandu, the capital of Nepal. Only the doctor could guess how ill she was. Everyone else thought she was going for a holiday and would soon be back.

'*I am not given long to live* . . .' Ruth wrote in 1976 from England to her friends back in Nepal. A very large tumour had been removed from her brain. Now it was growing again. '*But . . . the love of God is just as real to me as ever*,' she went on. Just over a month later, one of the Nepali nurses from the Shining Hospital had a dream. God was taking Ruth, the Kanchi Doctor, to be with him. The dream was true. Ruth had died.

Ruth's part in God's work in Nepal was over. But the work goes on. There is now a new, bigger hospital in Pokhara run jointly by the Nepali government and the missionaries. Many more people with leprosy are being treated. And God's family in Nepal is still growing. Wouldn't Ruth be glad about that?

God speaks your language

W Cameron Townsend

The mountain path was steep and his rucksack was heavy. 'Time for a rest,' thought the young American, and he sat down beside an old man who'd had the same idea. The man belonged to the Cakchiquel – one of the many Indian tribes who live in the Central American country of Guatemala.

'Good day,' said Cam, the American, speaking in Spanish, but the old Indian only grunted. Cam was not put off. He'd come to Guatemala to tell people that God loved them. His rucksack was full of the Spanish Bibles he was hoping to sell. This old man needed to hear what Cam had to say – but he only understood a little Spanish. At last he said in exasperation, 'If your God is so great, why can't he speak my language?' The words hit home to the American. It wasn't good enough to have Bibles in only certain languages. Everyone needed to hear God speaking in his own language.

William Cameron Townsend, or Cam as his family and friends called him, grew up on a little farm in California. He had four older sisters and a younger brother. They didn't have much money but there was plenty of fun and laughter in their poor home. Cam's father was deaf and his mother would often have to write out the joke so Dad could join in. Every morning, after breakfast, the whole family got together to pray, sing a hymn and read the Bible.

Cam was good at school. 'I think I'll be a teacher,' he decided. But in his final year he changed his plans. 'Could it be that God wants me to be a minister?' His parents were delighted with the idea and Cam enrolled at a college where he could study several subjects before starting the special training he would need to be the leader of a church.

Cam put down his book. He'd been reading about Hudson Taylor, the man who founded the China Inland Mission. 'Taylor dressed like the Chinese, ate Chinese food – became like a Chinese man in order to share God's love . . . he was a great man,' thought Cam. 'I'd try to be like him if God asked *me* to be a missionary.' Cam was thinking more and more about missionary work abroad. 'There are lots of ministers in the United States,' he reasoned. 'Couldn't God use me somewhere else?'

It was 1916. The First World War was raging in Europe, but America was not involved – yet. 'Did you know there's a man recruiting for the National Guard? Let's go and hear what he has to say.' Cam and his friend were impressed. 'Sounds like they give you really good training in engineering.' 'If America joins the war we'll be drafted into the services so we've nothing to lose by signing up now,' they decided.

Cam was still unsure about his future. Then one day he heard that men were needed to sell Spanish Bibles in South America. He'd studied Spanish.

Perhaps he could take a year off from college to see if he was cut out to work for God in a foreign country. 'They have accepted my application. I'm to go to Guatemala,' Cam told his parents, waving a letter from the Bible Society. But before Cam could set sail for Central America, the United States joined the war.

Corporal W. Cameron Townsend stood to attention before his officer in the National Guard. What would the officer think of the letter, a request from Cam's history professor that Cam be discharged from the army so that he could sell Bibles in Guatemala? It seemed unlikely that the officer would agree. Cam was fit and healthy and America was at war. He blinked in surprise at the officer's reply. He was free to go!

The ship dropped anchor outside the port and Cam and his friend Robbie got ready to leave. They had to get into a metal basket which swung them onto the tugboat. Soon they were through customs and on a train. They'd arrived in Guatemala at last.

'You'll be working in two adjoining towns where there's a group of Cakchiquel Indian Christians,' the older missionary told Cam. 'One of the Guatemalan pastors will walk there with you.' The road led at last over a hill and into a valley where Cam was shown his new home – a thatched hut with walls made out of bamboo and logs. There were some chickens to share his home and he was soon joined by many of the local Christians who had come to welcome him, for this hut was also their chapel. A few days later, Cam came across a scruffy looking Indian drinking beer. He sat down to talk to him and then offered him one of the little booklets he was carrying. It was the Gospel of John, part of the Bible.

'Sorry, I can't read,' replied the man. But as Cam was walking away, the Indian ran after him. He'd have the Gospel. His friend would read it to him. Then Cam had another idea.

'Why don't you come to the service in the chapel on Sunday?'

Cam looked round the crowded chapel. Women and children were sitting cross-legged on the floor. The men were on benches behind. Among them Cam spotted the man who had taken the Gospel booklet. When he started to preach, Cam tried to explain as clearly as he could how we can become God's friends. At the end of the service the man said he wanted to become a Christian. Cam was thrilled. This man, Tiburcio, was the first person he'd ever helped to meet Jesus.

Cam had one special Indian friend called Frisco. He agreed to go with Cam when he travelled to other villages to tell people of God's love. They went further and further afield, covering hundreds of miles in Guatemala, Honduras, El Salvador and Nicaragua. In the evenings, as they warmed themselves by a campfire, Frisco and Cam talked. The Indians had a hard life. Some worked as slaves on other men's land. Many were under the power of the witch-doctor. They had no schools and no one to tell them about God in their own language.

Cam knew the Cakchiquel language had never been written down. If he could find a way of writing it, he could translate the Bible for the Cakchiquel Indians. But it was a daunting task. Better start with something less impossible. 'A school?' Frisco's eyes lit up. 'A school in my home town. That would be wonderful!'

Cam's year in Guatemala was nearly up. He decided not to go home to finish his college course as he believed God had other work for him to do. But first he needed a rest. On holiday in Guatemala City, Cam was invited out to dinner. He found himself sitting next to an attractive young girl who was also a missionary. Cam and Elvira began to see more and more of each other. Could it be that Elvira shared Cam's dream of starting a school for the Indians? It seemed she did. Cam and Elvira were married and before long moved into a little hut next to the new school. There was one Indian teacher and about twenty pupils. It was small, but it was a start.

The school grew and so did Cam's schemes. There was a clinic, a children's home, a coffee-shelling machine so that the Indians could earn more from the coffee they grew, and a Bible Institute for training Indian church leaders. It wasn't surprising that Cam didn't have much time for what he most wanted to do – Bible translation.

The Cakchiquel language worked in a completely different way from English. 'Why should you say "one person" when you mean twenty and "two people" when you mean forty?' Cam wondered.

'Because each person has twenty fingers and toes!' came the reply.

'How can you explain "good neighbour" so that the Indians will understand?'

'How about "someone who will pick insects out of your hair without pulling it"?'

It was ten years after Cam first started to learn the language that the New Testament translation was completed. Elvira finished typing the manuscript – all but the last two words which Cam's parents proudly wrote in by hand. Now the Cakchiquel Indians could hear God speaking to them in their own language, but Cam was already thinking of the many thousands of others who needed Bible translators. 'I can't possibly do all the work myself,' Cam realised. 'But I could help to train others.'

'Camp Wycliffe' (later called the Summer Institute of Linguistics) was named after John Wycliffe, the man who, six hundred years earlier, had first translated the Bible into English. You needed to be tough to survive one of Cam's training camps – sleeping on hard boards with only grass cuttings as a mattress, sometimes going hungry, learning to listen to the tiny differences in pronunciation which could make a word mean 'black' instead of 'red'. Cam was pleased to see that one of his students was learning very quickly. 'I'm going to ask Ken Pike to teach,' he decided. God had sent along a man who was to become one of the very best linguists in the world.

The old car, pulling a sort of caravan, bumped along the cobbled streets of Tetelcingo. Cam and Elvira were in Mexico. They stopped the car and a group of Aztec Indian children gathered round. 'Where is the mayor?' Cam asked. A short, dark man approached. They spoke in Spanish. 'I have come to learn your language and to help the village people,' Cam said. 'Here are my official papers.'

Martin Mendez, the mayor of Tetelcingo, and Cam were soon good friends. One day, Martin asked to borrow a book. Cam was pleased to hand over the Spanish New Testament. As Martin read the book, he knew something strange was happening – he was changing! He stopped lying and getting drunk and beating his wife. The book was also teaching him to forgive his enemies. He bought three more copies of the New Testament and sent one to each of his three worst enemies. 'Perhaps they will read it and learn to forgive *me*,' he hoped.

The book was Cam's guide, too. He wanted to follow the example Jesus set. He hadn't come to Mexico to boss people about, but to help them. The Government was keen to make life better for the Indians, and the Indians were willing to help themselves. Before long, Tetelcingo could boast of piped water, a doctor, improved roads, a basketball court, vegetable gardens, and classes for adults and children where they could learn to read from books printed in Aztec and Spanish. Someone very important decided he must see this for himself.

'Why are those dogs barking?' Cam wondered and went to investigate. His heart jumped as he saw the man who had just got out of the big, black car and was now heading for the school. The President of Mexico!

'How does he know my name?' Cam thought as he and President Cardenas shook hands. He couldn't guess that before long he and the president would be the best of friends. Inside the school, the president talked to a big crowd of Indians who were waiting to see him. Later, he and Cam talked alone and Cam shared his dream of Bible translators for the Indians. 'Would they help in other ways?' wondered the president, looking over the vegetables Cam was growing. Cam assured him that they would and President Cardenas gave his approval.

The group of translators began to grow. By 1941 there were forty-four people working on tribal languages, but Cam knew that many, many more were needed. 'Let's ask God for another fifty,' he decided. With so many more people to train and support they would need a bigger camp site and a lot more money, but Cam believed that God could manage that! God gave even more than they asked for. The Wycliffe Bible Translators, as they now called themselves, had fifty-one new recruits by December 1942.

Cam knew his wife was ill. Elvira's heart had not been working properly for a long time. They were staying in a friend's house in California when she finally died. Cam was stunned and broken-hearted, but he was even more determined to carry on the work which Elvira and he had done together for so long.

Wycliffe Bible Translators had received a new invitation – this time to work in Peru. Twenty years earlier, Cam had dreamt of working in the Amazon jungle where many Indians lived. It seemed that now was the right time. Cam travelled thousands of miles by boat, canoe and plane, finding out all he could about the vast area of Amazonia. 'Some of the tribespeople will kill outsiders,' he was warned. But most of the Indians were friendly and Cam could see many ways to help them. If only their languages could be written down, then they could learn to read about better farming methods and ways to prevent the spread of disease. Best of all, they would be able to read what God was saying through the Bible. Before he left Peru to return to Mexico, Cam signed a contract with the government who were willing to help in Cam's next enormous job.

Cam hadn't planned to marry again, not for some time anyway. But it seemed that he was not to start work in Peru alone after all! Elaine. Lovely, blue-eyed Elaine who taught the Bible translators' children in Tetelcingo – Cam couldn't get her out of his mind! She was nearly twenty years younger than Cam. Would she agree to marry him? She did! President Cardenas was best man, paid for the wedding cake and offered his home for the ceremony. It was a grand setting for the wedding of a couple who would be starting their married life as hard-up missionaries in Peru.

Trips into the jungle could take weeks. Cam knew the Bible translators would have to do a lot of travelling. 'What we need is a plane that can land on water,' he decided. Then someone told him that the navy was selling off an amphibious plane. 'We'll call her "Amauta",' Cam decided. 'It means "a wise man at the service of the people".' He organised an official naming ceremony and invited important members of the Peruvian government and the American ambassador. The daughter of one of the government ministers held a horn filled with flower petals which she poured over the plane. The Peruvians were delighted and the ceremony was on the front pages of the newspapers. But Cam's contact with planes was not all happy.

Cam and Elaine had been visiting the jungle training camp in Mexico. Their family had increased and Grace, their little baby daughter, was lying in a basket on their knees as the small aircraft took off. The pilot made for a gap in the trees, but something went wrong. The plane lost height. Seconds later it crashed.

'Fire!' Cam's heart thumped., 'Will the plane catch fire? I must get the baby out.' Elaine's ankle was badly hurt and Cam had a broken leg but he was able to hand baby Grace to an Indian who ran up to the plane. Then some of the campers, who had been waving them off, arrived. A doctor saw to Elaine but before she was carried off on a stretcher Cam had an idea. One of the men had a cine camera. If he could take some pictures of the crash, people would see how much they needed safe aeroplanes for travelling in the jungle.

Recovering from the crash, with his leg in plaster, Cam had time to think. 'Could we set up a separate department of Wycliffe Bible Translators responsible for flying our missionaries?' It would need a lot of money and trained pilots and technicians but Cam was not put off. Before long the Jungle Aviation and Radio Service (JAARS) was operating in Peru.

More and more young people offered to give up their comfortable, safe lives to be Bible translators in the jungles of South America. Wycliffe carried on growing. So did Cam's family! His three daughters were at last joined by a son. 'I wish Daddy didn't have to go away again.' None of the family liked being separated. But Cam tried to make it up to them by writing letters, bringing back presents from his trips and playing wonderful games when he *was* at home. The children knew that their dad's work was really important. When people heard God speaking in their own language, they changed! One Indian chief became a follower of Jesus. He stopped fighting his enemies and asked them to live in peace instead.

It was seventeen years since Cam and Elaine had arrived in Peru. Now God was moving them on again – this time to Colombia. There were so many friends to leave behind, a large team of translators, Indians in the jungle and Government ministers. A special banquet was given in their honour. At last they were on the boat, steaming away from the shores of Peru – and Cam's face was wet with tears.

Uncle Cam (as most people called him by this time) had been in Colombia for three years when he had his seventieth birthday. But he wasn't retiring! Two years later he made his first trip to the Soviet Union and followed it up with ten more. He persuaded Russian officials that it would be a good idea to translate one book of the New Testament for some Soviet citizens who until then had had no part of the Bible in their language.

When Uncle Cam died in 1982 he left behind one of the largest Protestant missionary societies in the world. Wycliffe Bible Translators are working in all five continents and have just started work on their one thousandth language. Over two hundred New Testament translations have been completed and many shorter parts of the Bible. Their work will go on until they can say to every person in the world, 'God speaks *your* language.'

Not afraid to die

Janani Luwum

Janani looked up at the sky. Clouds were beginning to gather. 'Is rain coming?' he wondered. The grasslands around his African home in the north of Uganda went on for miles. There wasn't much to see. But the sky was always changing. Janani stared at the moving clouds, until a bleat and a scuffle brought him down to earth.

'Oh, no!' Don't say one of the goats has got loose again.' Janani ran as fast as his long legs would carry him and made a grab for the animal who had escaped from its tether. 'Back you come, silly old goat!' Janani breathed a sigh of relief. He knew he'd be in a lot of trouble if the goat got into their neighbour's field.

Janani didn't go to school. His father was a teacher in the church and he didn't earn enough for school fees. But Janani had plenty to do, chasing wild animals over the grassy plains, climbing trees with his friends, and looking after the family's sheep and goats and cows – when they had any.

'Why do we have to give her away?' Janani couldn't understand what his father was doing. 'She's the only cow we've got!' It was Christmas time and Janani's dad had made up his mind to give a special present to the church. 'I wish we could keep her,' Janani muttered to himself. A long time later he did understand why Dad had given the cow. When you really loved God you didn't want to keep things back from him. You had to be ready to give anything, do anything for him.

'He's bright, very bright.' Janani's teacher was pleased to see he was making up for lost time. He was ten and his parents had scraped together the money to send him to school. There was no stopping Janani now. When he finished at the local school, he went on to high school. It was eighty miles away, so he had to be a boarder. It meant *walking* all those miles at the beginning and end of term but it was worth it.

After high school, Janani became a student at teacher training college. He was coming to the end of his course and soon the students would know their final grades. 'This can't be right!' The education official from Kampala looked doubtfully at the grade given to Janani Luwum. 'No one can be that good. Perhaps the college has been too generous. We'd better send someone to check.' And so three people arrived to watch Janani teaching. The class sat spell-bound as he talked and drew pictures on the black-board to illustrate his story. No one mucked about when he had to take two classes for PE at the same time. The examiners were impressed. 'Yes,' they decided. 'He deserves the highest grade,'

'What's Mr. Luwum doing up a tree?' The children gathered round to hear what their teacher had to say. It was over three years since Janani had left college. He was a good teacher. Everyone respected him. Now something very exciting had happened to him. He had become a real follower of Jesus. He knew that Jesus had forgiven the wrong things he had done. He felt very happy inside and he wanted other people to be Jesus' friends, too. That's why he was preaching from the tree! But not everybody was happy with the new Janani.

A few weeks after he had given his life to Jesus, Janani was put in prison. Some of the church leaders, who should have known better, didn't like the things he'd been saying. They felt uncomfortable when he spoke out against wrong things which they would rather not have noticed. Janani was let out, but things were still hard. Then one day some friends put an idea to him. 'Would you be willing to give up your teaching job and become a pastor in the church?' To someone who loved teaching as much as Janani did, it was a hard thing to ask. People wouldn't think he was so important and he wouldn't get so much pay. Janani also knew that his parents expected him to become a village chief one day. But if this was what God wanted, he would do it.

So it was that Janani found himself a few years later four thousand miles from his Ugandan home. He'd arrived in London. By this time he had already trained to be a church leader and had been working with a church in Gulu in Northern Uganda. The bishop had picked him out as someone who could go far – and a year's study in England would help him. Janani shivered as the January wind whipped through his thin suit. He must get a thick coat. He wondered how Mary, his wife, and his children were. He missed them and a year was a long time to be apart.

Four years later he was back in Britain again for

more study. This time Mary was able to join him for some of the stay. Janani worked very hard and he found time to make lots of friends in England, too.

'We're going to have a new bishop – from our own people.' The members of the Acholi tribe in Northern Uganda were delighted. Janani was going to be a bishop. He had given up the chance to be a tribal chief, but God had another important job for him.

The thousands of people who crowded into the sports stadium, where the consecration ceremony was held, would never forget that day. President Obote and many other members of the Ugandan government were there. A police band played for the hymns. Christians in Northern Uganda had high hopes for their new leader. But Janani knew that God had not given him an easy job.

Just over a year later, Janani was back in the same sports stadium. He looked at the crowd of happy faces in front of him. Here were many people who had decided, in the last few days, to follow Jesus. Janani knew they would find it tough. He prayed specially that God would help them. But he did not realise just how much those new Christians would need God's help in the days to come.

On 25th January, 1971, the people of Uganda switched on their radios and heard some startling news. 'General Amin is in control.' The President was out of the country. He had gone to a conference in Singapore. Some people were pleased to have a new leader, but many were sad and frightened as they wondered what would happen next.

Crack! Crack! 'Is that gun-fire?' The people of Gulu, where Janani lived, woke to hear soldiers on the streets. 'Quick. Carry what you can. Let's get out of here!' Lots of people fled from the town. But even in the villages no one was safe. Many bodies were seen floating in the river.

During the next months, Janani travelled through Northern Uganda and in every village he visited there was heartbreak and the sound of mourners wailing for those who had died. He tried to do what he could to help those who had lost their husbands. 'Here is a little money from the church,' he would say. 'I'm sorry it can't be more. Let us try to forgive. Remember how Jesus forgave his enemies.'

Many Pakistani and Indian people were living in Uganda when General Amin took control. They worked hard and often ran successful businesses. Some African Ugandans resented this. The General decided they must go. He didn't mind *where*, so long as they got out of Uganda. He didn't see that Uganda would be much poorer without them. Janani was in Holland when he first heard the news that the Asians had to go. He did not agree with General Amin and Amin knew it. 'What will happen when I get home?' Janani wondered.

Some of Janani's friends were afraid that he might be arrested, but for now he was free – free to do his work of caring for Christians and free to do all he could to persuade people to come to know and love God. Then he was asked to leave Gulu. He had been elected as the new Archbishop of the Church of Uganda.

It was a great honour, but Janani felt sad. He didn't want to leave the people he loved in Northern Uganda. And his new job brought many responsibilities – one of them to speak out against things that were wrong.

Things were very wrong in Uganda, and getting worse. Janani was often asked to help when a husband went missing. Was he dead, or still alive in prison? Janani would try to find out and sometimes got the man released.

People were afraid to go out after dark. It became hard to get food and water. For a while, petrol was in short supply and a hospital was only allowed to use one of its ambulances. Students at the university who protested because one of their wardens had been killed, were made to crawl through the mud. Amin's soldiers even made some of them jump out of high windows.

'We must speak out against these terrible things,' Janani decided. 'We will invite all the church leaders to a meeting.' The lawns of the conference centre, where the meeting was held, ran down to a sparkling lake. There were peanuts and bananas to eat and coffee to drink. It was a beautiful setting in which to discuss the ugly things that were happening in Uganda.

'Ordinary people are being arrested by the military police.'

'People are afraid that if their names are on the black list, they will be taken away and perhaps tortured and killed.'

'Some of the officials who are supposed to make sure that supplies are given out fairly are cheating to make money for themselves. Poor people can't afford to pay the high "black market" prices.'

'We should ask to see President Amin to tell him

about the things that are troubling us.'

A record was made of everything that was discussed at the meeting. At the bottom was the chairman's signature, 'Janani Luwum'.

President Amin did not agree to meet the church leaders. He was furious. No one had asked his permission to have the meeting. He wanted to see the written record of what had been said. As he read it, he got more and more angry. Then he looked with hatred at the name at the bottom of the record.

On New Year's Eve, 1976, Janani and some other Christians climbed the hill to the cathedral in Kampala. Far away, they could hear drums beating to welcome the new year. 1977 was a special year. It was a hundred years since missionaries had first come to tell the people of Uganda the good news of Jesus. Janani and the others read from the Bible – it was a psalm written by David. He, too, had gone through hard times. He, too, had almost given up. But David knew, and the little group of Christians sitting outside the cathedral knew, that the safest place to be was close to God.

Little more than a month later, Janani was woken in the middle of the night. 'Why is the dog barking?' he wondered. 'Is someone getting over the fence?' His heart thumped as he went to investigate. He could see a man outside – someone he recognised. There was blood on his face. But before Janani could get to the injured man, he felt a rifle butt being pushed against him.

Three armed men started to search the house. They looked everywhere: under mattresses, in suitcases, even in the sack of peanuts Mary kept in the food store. They were looking for guns. But they didn't find any. Janani didn't agree with many things the president was doing but he still prayed for Amin and he wasn't going to be involved in getting rid of him by force.

'The Archbishop's house has been raided!' The story of what had happened quickly spread. Everyone was shocked. 'We must tell the president how we feel,' the church leaders decided. They wrote a message to President Amin complaining about the terrible things that were happening: the killing of innocent people; the raid on the Archbishop's house; the persecution of people who had been to university.

Fifteen bishops wrote their names at the bottom of the message. 'We will all deliver it to President Amin,' they vowed. But the president did not reply to their request to see him. Then he sent a message to Janani. 'He will see me by myself,' Janani told his wife. Mary's heart was gripped with fear. 'Please don't go,' she begged. But Janani knew he must be willing to risk his own life for the people of Uganda. In the end, both he and Mary went to the President's house.

President Amin sipped his tea and looked with contempt at Janani. 'You are plotting to overthrow my government,' he said, 'Some children found boxes of arms near your home.' Janani knew it wasn't true but he couldn't argue with the president. Later that day, he went home with a heavy heart.

The next afternoon, a message came to Janani's office. 'There is going to be a big meeting tomorrow morning. President Amin is going to speak to members of the government, the army and church leaders.' 'What does it mean?' Janani's friends wondered.

Janani and six bishops got to the meeting in good time. A big crowd of people were waiting for them, but no one greeted them with a friendly face. Janani's eyes grew wide as he saw the cases of guns and bullets on show. Reporters from foreign newspapers and radio stations had been invited. 'This isn't an ordinary meeting,' the bishops realised. 'This is a trial – our trial.'

Someone read from papers which were supposed to be written by President Obote, the man Amin had replaced when he made himself president. They included plans for getting rid of Amin, plans to smuggle guns and ammunition over the border from Kenya to be sent eventually to Archbishop Luwum. Janani knew this wasn't true, but there was nothing he could say. He was not afraid to die. He remained silent, just as Jesus had been at his trial before Pontius Pilate. Then the man in charge of the trial asked the soldiers what should happen to the church leaders. Everyone said they should be killed.

The bishops expected to die very soon. But it seemed they were not to face the firing squad after all. They were taken into a small room inside the conference centre. 'Wait in here,' they were told and one of Amin's men was left to guard them. At last they could hear clapping. The president must have finished his speech. Then to their surprise, they were told they could go . . . but not all of them. Janani must stay to see the president, alone.

Two of Janani's bishop friends stood by his car. 'Why is the president keeping him so long?' 'What's happening to him?,' they wondered. 'When will he be free?' They didn't know that they would never see their friend on earth again. Sadly, they made their way back to Janani's house after the soldiers had forced them to leave.

On 17th February, 1977 the people of Kampala read their newspapers in shock and disbelief. 'It says the Archbishop has been killed in a car crash!' No one was taken in by the photographs that appeared in the newspapers. The smashed-up car, where Janani was supposed to have died, had been involved in an accident some days earlier. When Janani's body was seen in the mortuary there were three bullet holes. Some say he prayed for his murderers as he died.

Janani's funeral was to take place the following Sunday. Outside the cathedral, men dug a grave. But the authorities would not produce the body. Then Janani's friends received another blow. The news quickly got around, 'We are not allowed to hold the memorial service in Kampala.' But when Sunday came, no one could stop the thousands of Christians who made their way up the hill to the cathedral.

The service ended, but no one wanted to go home. Outside the cathedral people began to sing a hymn. Everyone was thinking of Janani who had died because he was following Jesus. And there was Janani's grave, still empty. As they looked at it, people began to think of another grave that was empty – Jesus' grave on Easter morning. Smiles started to appear on sad faces. Janani had died, but now he was alive. He was alive with Jesus!

A hundred years in God's army

Catherine Bramwell-Booth

'No one wants you when you're old. What good am I now?' thought the white-haired lady. She looked sadly out over her quiet, English garden and talked to God. He would understand. But only a day later Catherine Bramwell-Booth was in for a surprise. She was turned ninety, but God still had exciting work for her to do. 'The BBC want to interview me!' she gasped. 'I'm going to be on television!'

Catherine watched, fascinated, as the recording equipment, cameras and arc lights were brought into the sitting room. There were electric cables everywhere. But she wasn't put off by the paraphernalia. The interview was a success. Catherine was invited to London to appear on a TV chat show. All over the country, people listened in amazement to this sprightly old lady as she shared some of her memories from her fascinating life.

When Catherine's grandfather, William Booth, came to London in 1865, he saw crowds of poor people. Many of them did not know of God's love. They spent what little money they had on getting drunk, and some even had to sleep on the streets. He longed to tell them that Jesus could change them so that they wouldn't need to get drunk to escape from their miseries. Others joined him in his work and soon there were many people caring for those who were ill or poor and preaching the good news of Jesus. They called themselves 'The Salvation Army'. Soon they were well known: marching along the streets in their smart uniforms singing hymns with a brass band often leading the procession.

William Booth was the Army's General. People flocked to hear him. Many became Christians. But some didn't like The Salvation Army and made fun of its 'soldiers'. William's son, Bramwell, and daughter-in-law, Florence, were both members of the Army and so when their first child, Catherine, arrived in 1883, it seemed she was born to be a soldier!

The Salvation Army soldiers may have been having a tough time on the streets, but for Catherine, life was safe and peaceful. She had lots of happy times – snuggling into bed with Mama and Papa as a special treat; riding on the top of an open-topped double decker bus pulled by horses; running to buy muffins from a man balancing a big tray on top of his head.

Catherine didn't go to school. Instead, she and her sisters and brother sat at a big table in their home and Mama was their teacher. 'What are nine sixes, Cath?'

'Oh, no, let me think . . .' Numbers were not one of Catherine's strong points! One of the things she *did* enjoy was listening to her mother reading stories aloud. They would all lie on the floor and Mama's clear voice would drift over them, taking them into many different worlds.

Near Catherine's house there were fields to be explored when lessons were over. Catherine and her sisters would run and play and make new discoveries. 'Look, Cath! The frog spawn we saw last week has turned into tadpoles! Some of them are even beginning to get legs. Can you see?' At home they kept many pets: an Irish terrier, rats, guinea pigs and mice. When Catherine was much older and at The Salvation Army's training college, a certain mouse caused quite a stir. . . . But more about that later!

As Catherine was growing up, so was The Salvation Army. There were so many people who needed help and needed to hear about Jesus. One night, William Booth was walking across London Bridge. 'What are those shapes at the side of the pavement?' he wondered. Then he realised they were people – people sleeping out in the cold, night air. 'If we could provide a warm warehouse for them, it would be better than nothing,' General Booth decided. And soon The Salvation Army's first shelter for homeless people was started.

While some people had no homes, many others had no jobs. Those who did have work often had to put up with terrible conditions inside their factories. People who made matches invariably got 'phossy-jaw' when they came into contact with phosphorus. Phossy-jaw gave you dreadful toothache and your teeth would eventually drop out. The Salvation Army gave safe work to many people in a factory where matches were made *without* using phosphorus.

When Catherine was nearly seven years old, she was taken on a very special outing to the glittering glass building in South London called the Crystal Palace. Fifty thousand people gathered to celebrate an anniversary. It was twenty-five years since

Catherine's grandfather, General Booth, had first started preaching in East London. The brass bands played and the people inside and outside the palace sang and sang. Catherine would never forget it.

Later that year, Catherine was taken to another big occasion, but this one was very sad. Her grandmother, General Booth's wife, had died. Thousands of people stood on the streets of London to watch the funeral procession. Catherine and her sisters sat in one of the open horse-drawn carriages following the coffin. It must have been exciting to ride through the streets with so many people looking on. But Catherine's thoughts were sad. 'Grandmama is dead. Oh, Grandmama, I did love you so much!'

Grandpapa Booth now lived alone in a house not far from Catherine's. He was still very busy travelling round the country, but when he was at home, he liked to see his grandchildren. There was a tradition that early on Christmas day they would sing carols to him whilst he was still in his bedroom.

One Christmas morning, the children were feeling inside their stockings to see what goodies were inside. Everyone was happy and excited. 'What's this right in the toe?' 'I've got a tangerine.' 'Look Cath! Just what I wanted.' 'What have you got?' Suddenly Grandpapa's voice boomed up the stairwell. He was singing a carol! They had forgotten to come to him, so he had come to them instead.

When Grandpapa came to tea, Catherine loved to hear him and her father talking about the Army. She would sit very still at the tea table, listening to their conversation. She knew she would have to leave if they remembered she was there. Everything in

Catherine's family revolved round the Army. She longed for the day when she could be a soldier herself.

Birthdays were always exciting. But Catherine was looking forward more than ever to her next one. For then she would be twelve years old – old enough to join her local corps of The Salvation Army. Once in the Army, Catherine began to play the tenor horn. It was wonderful to put on her smart, navy blue uniform and to march through the streets with the band. But a soldier's duties are more than being on parade. Catherine visited people who were ill and she began to see how children could suffer when their parents drank too much.

Being General Booth's granddaughter had its advantages. Sometimes Grandpapa would take Catherine with him when he went on preaching tours. But Catherine found it had drawbacks too.

'Why do people expect me to do things well just because I'm a Booth?' she wondered. 'It doesn't seem fair. I'm not very good at singing, and I hate talking in front of lots of people. I can only do my best . . .' But Grandpapa taught her an important lesson. God could help Catherine to do *better* than her best!

As a teenager, Catherine never really wondered what she would do when she was old enough to have a job. She just knew that one day she would be a Salvation Army officer. As the time for her to go to the Army's training college came closer, Catherine felt a mixture of excitement and dread. 'It will mean leaving behind everything and everyone I love,' she thought. But in the years to come God would give Catherine many, many other people to love.

Life at college was tough and Catherine *did* feel

homesick. She was looking forward to a visit from some of her younger sisters though she didn't know about another visitor they were planning to bring.

'Let's take Cath's mouse with us,' they decided. 'That should give her a nice surprise.' It did! Mice had always been Catherine's favourite pets. 'Perhaps I could keep it here, just for a while,' she mused. And so the mouse lived inside her uniform, sleeping in the dip made by her collar bone. That was until it decided to take a look at the outside world!

The cadets were listening carefully to their teacher. Catherine, too, was trying to concentrate on the lecture when she felt her mouse's soft hair brushing against her skin. 'Oh no! Don't say it's waking up!' One of the other girls began to giggle, another let out a scream as she saw the pointed nose and beady eyes peeping over Catherine's collar. Soon the whole class were joining in and the teacher had to stop the lecture to find out what all the fuss was about. It may not have been the sort of thing the Army General's granddaughter should be up to, but Catherine was thoroughly enjoying herself.

After college, Catherine was posted to her first corps, in Bath. She was expected to be able to take charge, to stand up and speak in front of people. It wasn't easy! Her knees might feel like jelly, but she had to put on a brave face and keep going. She also had to learn how to deal with men who would call out and try to compete with the person who was preaching.

When Catherine was in her first posting, Grand-papa Booth began to make use of a new invention – the motor car! He travelled hundreds of miles and spoke at meetings all over the country. Catherine was very excited when she heard that he was going to make a tour of the West of England. She could hardly wait to tell people the news. 'He's coming to Bath, and he'll take me with him on his tour.'

It was marvellous to sit beside Grandpapa in the big open car. William Booth was a famous man and lots of people stood beside the road to watch him go past.

'Stop the car, please, driver,' he would say from time to time. Then he would stand up in the back of the car and speak to the little groups of people who gathered round.

Grandpapa was already an old man. Over the next few years his sight began to fail. When he was eighty three he spoke at a special birthday celebration in the Royal Albert Hall. Although he was old and nearly blind, he told the people that he was still a fighter in God's army, fighting to give poor people a better life and to show them that God loved them. Not long afterwards this 'old soldier' finished his fight.

The streets of London were crowded with people for General Booth's funeral procession, just as they had been when his wife died. There were as many people as you might see at a royal wedding nowadays.

'Will The Salvation Army keep going without William Booth?' people wondered. It certainly did! Catherine's father, Bramwell Booth, became the next General. Two years later, he and The Salvation Army were to face a new and frightening challenge.

When the First World War began in 1914, there were Salvation Army officers in Germany as well as in Britain. They knew they were all members of God's family. Could they be expected to fight and kill each other? Bramwell Booth planned ways for The Salvation Army to help the fighting men without taking sides in the war. They supplied ambulances to take wounded men from the 'Front Line' to hospitals and they ran canteens for the soldiers.

During the war, Catherine was one of the teachers at The Salvation Army Training College. There were no men there – they were all away at the war. But hundreds of young women came to be trained. Catherine's job was to talk to each of the cadets by themselves and to see if they had any problems. If one of the girls said, 'I'm frightened of talking in front of people,' Catherine knew just how she felt! She remembered her own knocking knees and thumping heart. If God had helped her, she knew he would help these girls, too.

At the end of the war, Germany's army was defeated and many of her people were poor and hungry. Catherine's father looked up sadly from the report he was reading.

'Some children in Germany cannot even stand up because they are so weak from lack of food,' he said. 'We must do something to help.'

Then The Salvation Army received a large sum of money from the Save the Children Fund. 'They want us to use the money to help poor children in Berlin,' Bramwell explained to Catherine. 'I'd like you to organise the relief work.'

It was wonderful to be helping the children. They quickly began to get strong again as they drank their milk and swallowed spoonfuls of cod-liver oil. And Catherine had a wonderful experience when she visited Germany. It was at a big Salvation Army meeting in Hamburg. For four years the British and German people had been at war. Millions had died and there was still much bitterness and hatred. But when Catherine arrived at the meeting she had a marvellous reception. It didn't matter that she was British and the others were German. They were all friends and children of the same Heavenly Father.

For years Catherine had been a very busy person. She had done lots of very hard things. But when she weas nearly forty, she had to do something even harder. She had to stay in bed for almost a year. There was something badly wrong with both her lungs and the doctor said she must have complete rest.

'Why has God let this happen?' she thought miserably. 'Will I ever be able to work again?' The doctor thought she might die, but to everyone's surprise, she began to get better. A few months in Switzerland helped to get her back on her feet and at last the great day came when she was well enough to start work again.

Another new job! Catherine loved a challenge. This time she was to be in charge of helping women who were in all sorts of trouble. A teenage girl might have run away from home and then been taken to court for stealing something. Rather than put her in prison, the court could send her to a Salvation Army hostel for a few months. Whatever had made the girl do bad things, Catherine knew that the one sure way a person's life can be put right is by starting to follow Jesus. Lots of the girls did just that and when they came back to visit the hostel, happily married with children of their own, Catherine would know that her hard work had been worthwhile.

Catherine was still very nervous of speaking in public but she certainly had plenty of practice! Her next job was to travel all over Europe, taking meetings, speaking to the Salvation Army's officers and encouraging the cadets who were still in training. Although she was nervous to begin with, once she had started to talk, Catherine would often get a thrill of excitement as she saw people on the edge of their seats, eager to hear what she had to say. The great thing was to surprise them, not to let them get bored.

Being with Salvationists in other countries was wonderful, *getting there* was not such fun. Catherine was a terrible sailor. 'Oh, to stand on dry land!' she would cry to herself as the boat lurched up and down in the strong sea. Sometimes she was too ill to walk off the boat when it finally docked. Imagine her delight when she first travelled from Norway by air. All the way over the North Sea without being sick! Marvellous!

As Catherine travelled through Europe, she didn't realise that soon the peace would be shattered with the outbreak of the Second World War. Once again, Salvation Army officers were involved in helping the soldiers: running hostels where they could stay when they were on leave, visiting the injured in hospital, sometimes speaking to those who were dying.

One of Catherine's sisters was arrested and put in a camp for prisoners of war. There she was able to encourage the other prisoners and to read the Bible to them. After the war The Salvation Army worked to bring together husbands and wives, parents and children, and brothers and sisters who had been separated because of the fighting.

Three years after the end of the war it was Catherine's sixty-fifth birthday. This was a birthday she was not looking forward to because The Salvation Army rules said she must retire. Retire! It was unthinkable. Catherine had so much energy. She couldn't sit around all day doing nothing. And indeed she didn't. Although her official work was over, for the next thirty years she was still busy, speaking at meetings, writing and keeping up to date with news of The Salvation Army.

Then, in her nineties, Catherine began to feel that she really *was* no longer needed. Until, that was, she had the phone call from the BBC. After her television and radio interviews, letters came pouring in from all over the country. She had now spoken to a bigger audience than ever before. Life in God's army is certainly full of surprises!

Five bullets for the bishop

H. B. Dehqani-Tafti

It was still early in the morning, but already the people of Taft were waking up. From the village mosque, the muezzin was calling the people to say their prayers. Four year old Hassan stirred and stretched on the mat where he had been sleeping on the roof of his house. The start of another day. Soon he would be playing in the village square with his older brother and the other children. 'I hope Yahya will let me join in today,' he thought.

After breakfast, Hassan ran barefoot up the narrow, dusty streets to join the others in the village square. There was no danger of being knocked down by a car. Cars were only just appearing in the big cities of Iran in the 1920s. No one in Taft owned one. Only the donkey carts had to be avoided as the children chased each other round the square.

The morning passed quickly and soon Hassan's stomach was telling him it was time for lunch. When he got back home he was not surprised to see that several people were crowding into the little house. His home always seemed to be full of people who had come to his mother for help. Hassan's mother was a nurse and in one room she kept her supplies of medicines, bandages and disinfectant.

There was no doctor's surgery or clinic for the people of Taft to go to. But, when she was younger, Mrs Dehqani, Hassan's mother, had trained as a nurse at a hospital in the nearest big town. The hospital was run by Christian missionaries and it was while she was working there that Hassan's mother had first learnt about Jesus and decided that she wanted to follow him. It wasn't easy for her to let people know that she was a Christian. Everyone else in Taft, and almost everyone else in the whole of Iran, was a Muslim – and Muslims are not allowed to change their faith.

Life was good for Hassan. As well as his older brother, he had a younger brother and just recently they'd had a new baby sister. But before long his happy world was shattered. Mum was ill. She had a dreadful cough so she didn't sleep on the roof with the rest of the family. One morning Hassan came down-stairs and looked around.

'Where's Mum?' he asked. But Mum was not there. She had died during the night and Hassan's life would never be the same again.

As the months went by, Hassan became aware that his father was having an argument with a lady who often called at their house. Miss Kingdom was a foreigner, an English missionary, and she was a very determined person!

'How can you expect me to let Hassan be taught by people who are not Muslims?' Father was saying. 'It's out of the question.' But Miss Kingdom did not give up.

'You know it was your wife's dying wish that he

73

should be brought up as a Christian. She would be so happy to know that he was at a Christian school.'

Father was not convinced. He would have to see the Mullah, the Muslim teacher, and ask him to look in the Muslim's holy book called the Koran. People often did that when they had a hard decision to make. Miss Kingdom waited to see what would happen. She was delighted when Mr Dehqani told her the result of the 'consultation'. 'It is good,' he said. 'Hassan may go to the Christian school.'

'It will mean leaving Taft,' Hassan realised. He would miss playing with his friends in the village square, helping in the blacksmith's shop where his uncle and grandfather worked, and driving the sheep to drink at the pool outside the village. It was the beginning of a new life.

Hassan and his father walked fifteen miles across the desert to Yezd, the nearest big town to Taft. They walked through the night because it was cooler. Sometimes Father had to carry six year old Hassan on his shoulders.

At the Christian school, Hassan learned to write the Persian alphabet and heard stories from the Bible. He was happy there. But the school was really for girls. Once he was seven, he would have to leave. During the summer holidays, there were more discussions between Father and Miss Kingdom. Eventually Father agreed to let Hassan go to the Christian boys' school, two hundred miles away in Isfahan.

Isfahan. Hassan had heard of it, of course. It was said to be the most beautiful city in the whole of Iran, with its famous blue mosque and ancient palaces, now joined by smart new buildings. But when he saw it for himself, he could hardly believe his eyes. It was even more spectacular than he had imagined. And this beautiful city was to be his home for the next ten years.

'Your writing is really excellent,' said the head-master. He was full of praise for Hassan. It wasn't surprising that it began to go to the boy's head. Hassan knew that he was a favourite. Being good at calligraphy and poetry and learning Bible stories had helped. He liked school. This was where he felt at home. But it wasn't his home, was it? In the summer holidays he would go back to Taft, to his father and brothers and the Muslim friends he had left behind. It took a lot of getting used to. He almost felt like a different person.

At school, Hassan learned about Jesus. He made up his mind that he wanted to become a Christian. But his family in Taft were not happy with the news. One summer holiday, Father put his foot down.

'You're not going back to Isfahan,' he told his dejected son. 'You can go to the village school run by the Mullah.' But after one day there, Hassan refused to go again and went instead to a government school – but not for long.

Letters began to arrive, some from Miss Kingdom and some from the headmaster of the Christian school. Would Father change his mind and allow Hassan to return to Isfahan? He decided to consult the Koran and, to Hassan's great joy, the answer was once again 'Yes'.

By the time he was seventeen, Hassan knew for sure that he wanted to be baptised as a Christian. He knew his father would be sad. It was a disgrace for the whole family to have a son change his religion. Hassan sent a letter to his father to try to explain how he felt. He wrote, *'I have found the joy and happiness I want in Jesus Christ'*. Back in Taft, people he had known would look the other way when they passed him in the street. It was hard to be a Christian, but it was worth it.

The Second World War was raging by the time Hassan went to university in Tehran. In spite of the hours spent queueing in the shop for bread, and the hard work of studying for exams, Hassan enjoyed being a student. He certainly preferred it to being a soldier – but there was no escape from military training when he left university.

Guard duty again. Hassan groaned. As the hours passed, he shifted his weight from one foot to the other and stared ahead. There was no fighting in Tehran. Boredom was the main problem. Then Hassan began to remember the words of Psalms he had learnt years ago at school. Some of them he made into poems in Persian and these were later sung as hymns by Iranian Christians.

As he spoke both Persian and English, Hassan's last job in the army was to interpret for an American colonel. He carried on with this job even after he was discharged from the army. It was interesting and the pay was *very* good. His family were pleased.

'Perhaps all this education has been worthwhile,' they thought. They looked forward to receiving some of Hassan's high wages. But they were soon to be disappointed. 'How can I expect them to understand?' Hassan wondered. He was planning to give up his well paid job to train to be a church leader. He knew it meant cutting himself off from his family and he didn't want that. But he believed God was asking him to be a Christian leader and he must say yes. Hassan enjoyed working in the church: doing things with the other young people, selling Christian books and learning all he could. He was very excited when the Church decided that he should go to England to study.

'Is it really happening?' Hassan thought as he looked around the beautiful old college buildings, the lush green lawns and the river where some students were punting. 'Am I really a student in Cambridge?' He thought back to Taft, the little Muslim village that had once been his home. The two places were worlds apart.

Few people guessed that Hassan Dehqani, the bright new Theology student, was really very unhappy. Secretly he still missed his mother who had died so long ago, and now he was cut off from his father and the rest of his family. 'Why has God let all this happen to me?' he thought miserably. He was very grateful to a wise Christian man who listened to his troubles and helped him to trust in God's help for each day and not to worry about the future. Back in Iran, God helped Hassan in another way. He gave him a lovely wife, Margaret, and a family of his own.

Only a few years after returning to his own country, Hassan was made a bishop. For twenty years or so he was busy leading the small Christian church in Iran. There may have been only a few Christians, but they were responsible for two hospitals and two clinics, boarding schools for boys and girls, schools for blind children and a centre where blind men could learn to be farmers.

Hassan and Margaret were proud of their growing family. Their son, Bahram, went to boarding school in England and then to universities in England and America. Shiran, their eldest daughter, had also been studying in America, Suzanne was training to be a nurse in London and Guli was a school girl in Iran. In 1978, Hassan was asked to attend a conference of bishops in London. 'Wouldn't it be good to have a family reunion?' he suggested. And so the Dehqani family were all together in England when they began to hear worrying news from Iran.

'There have been more demonstrations and riots in Tehran.'

'Shops have been looted.'

'A cinema full of people has been set on fire.' The television news went from bad to worse. The Iranian people were letting everyone know that they had had enough of their ruler, the Shah. Instead, they wanted to be governed by their Muslim leader, the man who had been forced to leave the country, the Ayatollah Khomainy.

'Where will it all lead?' Hassan wondered. 'Will the Christians be harmed?' He knew he must get back to Iran as quickly as possible.

People were speaking out fearlessly against the Shah. Even the headquarters of his dreaded secret police force was attacked. Life in Iran was getting more and more chaotic. There was sometimes no electricity, the post office workers were on strike, food and petrol were in short supply. At last the Shah was forced to flee the country and in February, 1979, the Ayatollah Khomainy came home to a *very* enthusiastic welcome.

The members of the Anglican Church in Iran were pleased that the Shah's regime had come to an end. Like everyone else, they hoped that life would be fairer and happier now. As the leader of the church, Hassan wrote a welcoming letter to the Ayatollah Khomainy. But it was soon obvious that it would not be easy for these Christians to live with the Islamic revolution.

Two of Hassan's friends came to see him. They had bad news. One of the Iranian priests was dead. 'Murdered in his office . . . his son found the body,' they told Hassan. Two men were suspected of being the murderers, but the police allowed them to go free.

Soon after, the church leaders were meeting together to pray and think about their work.

'It seems we are living in dangerous times. Perhaps some of us will even have to die for our faith,' Hassan told the others. 'Pray about what you should do. If you decide you must leave Iran, you will be free to go.' But the church leaders all said they would stay. Then they prayed for God's help in all that was to come.

It wasn't long before the church members received more bad news. Men from the 'Revolutionary Committee' had arrived at the Christian hospital in Isfahan. They had banned the Christians from telling others about Jesus. Now some of the men wanted to say how the hospital should be run, even though they knew nothing about hospitals or about medicine. The next target of the men from the Isfahan Revolutionary Committee was the school for blind boys. The Christian missionaries who worked there were all forced to leave. The other Christian hospital in Shiraz was also taken over. 'What next?' Hassan wondered.

One hot day in August, Hassan and Margaret had just got up from their afternoon nap. Suddenly the door burst open and a group of men raided the house. They were noting where the kitchen was, and the study and the bedroom. Why should they want to know that? When they had left, Hassan and Margaret looked to see what had been taken.

'The photograph albums,' cried Margaret. 'Why should they want photographs of our children? And the letters Suzanne wrote from London. They're missing, too!'

'So are some important lists of names,' Hassan noticed. 'Why should they want to know who receives my monthly letter?' The raid left the couple badly shaken – and worse was to come.

A few weeks later, four men pulled up in a van outside the Dehqani's house. They called themselves revolutionary guards and they had come to arrest the bishop. At their headquarters, Hassan was locked in a little room where there was a pillow, a blanket, and a chair. 'How long will I be here?' he wondered. Unknown to him, a message was on its way from the authorities in Tehran. The bishop must be released. And so, to his great relief, Hassan was told he was free to go. But he wasn't out of danger yet.

Before long, Hassan was summoned to answer questions from a revolutionary court. They accused the foreign missionaries who worked with the Iranian Christians of being spies. They complained because the bishop had met the British and American ambassadors. But they didn't detain Hassan. Once again he was free to go.

'What's happening?' Hassan woke at the sound of his wife's voice. He opened his eyes and found himself looking straight into a revolver. 'It's over,' he thought as the shots rang out. 'No more worry. I'm going to die.' But moments later, he heard running footsteps. Margaret was chasing the gunmen. He must still be alive!

Gingerly Hassan felt to see if his head was bleeding. No. Everything was all right. Perhaps they hadn't been real bullets in the revolver. But when Margaret returned from chasing the men, he saw her hand was bleeding badly. It had been hit by a bullet. Looking at his pillow, Hassan saw the holes made by four more bullets. Each one had narrowly missed his head.

You could say he was lucky to be alive. But Hassan knew that it was God who had protected him. Days after the assassination attempt, he and Margaret had to leave the country for a church conference in Cyprus. He didn't mean to be away for long, but all his friends gave him the same advice – 'Don't come back yet.'

It was getting harder and harder for members of the Anglican Church in Iran. People were spreading lies about them, forging letters as evidence that they were spies. If Hassan returned to his home, he would almost certainly be killed. And so it was decided that Margaret should go back alone to be with the children while Hassan stayed in Egypt and then in Cyprus.

It wasn't long before Hassan heard more sad news. Gunmen had shot his secretary, Jean Waddell, in a flat in Tehran. They had left her for dead, but, miraculously, she was alive and was now recovering in hospital. Margaret was at her bedside.

Hassan and Margaret were learning to live with trouble. But they didn't know that the hardest test of all was soon to come. Hassan was at a conference in Cyprus. One night there was a knock at his bedroom door. He was wanted on the phone. Rubbing the sleep from his eyes, with his heart racing, he hurried down the corridor. What could it be? Who would want to speak to him at this time? Minutes later, he put the phone down, as if in a trance. Bahram, his twenty-four year old son, was dead. He had been shot in Iran.

Hassan wept for the son he'd loved so dearly. 'They killed him instead of me,' he thought. 'Because I wasn't there . . .' In his grief, Hassan prayed that God would bring something good out of the terrible tragedy. And he prayed that God would forgive the men who had killed his son.

After Bahram's death, his parents received many letters from all over the world. One of Bahram's Iranian friends wrote:

'When Christ lived among men I was not there to see him,

But now and then we get glimpses of him shown to us through other people;

I saw him in Bahram.'

Hassan and Margaret are now living in exile in England. Their small church in Iran has survived, but it is not yet safe for Hassan to return.

A man who went missing

Richard Wurmbrand

'Will you wait for me? I have a message to deliver.' The two friends were on their way home from school in the Turkish city of Istanbul. Eight year old Richard had never been inside a place like this before. Full of curiosity, he peered round the old building until his friend reappeared with the white bearded priest. 'He's got a kind face,' thought Richard. Even so, he was surprised when the old man asked if there was anything he wanted.

'N-no thank you,' replied Richard. But the priest insisted. 'Well, could I have some water, please, sir?'

'Of course, son,' said the priest and hurried off to get it. This unexpected kindness stuck in Richard's mind. Maybe that's why he was still fascinated by churches long after he'd decided that God was not really there at all.

Richard was born in Rumania, a European country bordered by Bulgaria, Yugoslavia, Hungary, the Soviet Union and the Black Sea. His father was a dentist and Richard was the youngest of a family of four boys. When he was only five years old, the First World War began. At first, his country was on the German side, but later changed to support the British and the French.

Times were very hard for the Rumanian people. (That's why Richard's father had taken his family for a short time to live in Turkey.) Things got even worse for Richard's family when his father died of 'flu. They were always hungry and had to wear shabby clothes. But one thing they were *not* short of was books.

'Reading again, Richard?' Mum knew she would find her youngest son with his head in one of his father's books. The trouble was, he tended to believe everything he read. It wasn't long before Richard had made up his mind that the books were right – it was stupid to believe in God.

Since he didn't have to worry about pleasing God, as a young man, Richard did everything to please himself. He was bright and full of energy and had soon made a lot of money.

He was tall and good looking and had plenty of girlfriends.

'Don't you think it's time you settled down and found yourself a wife?' his mother would say. 'I know of a girl from a very rich family.' Richard was not impressed with his mother's choice! But when his uncle brought Sabina, a pretty, dark-haired student, to the house Richard felt differently. Like Richard, Sabina came from a Jewish family. But neither she nor Richard had any time for God. All they wanted was to enjoy themselves as much as possible and so they spent their evenings going the rounds of parties, dances and night clubs.

The couple had been married for less than a year when Richard became ill with a terrible cough. As he walked out of the doctor's surgery, he felt his world crumbling. How could he break the news to Sabina? He had tuberculosis (TB), which in the 1930s was a killer disease.

The only hope of a cure for TB was rest and fresh air. So Richard left the busy city of Bucharest and went to a special hospital called a sanatorium in the Carpathian mountains. There he had plenty of time to think, and to feel very frightened. He was afraid of dying. He was afraid that God would not be pleased about the bad things he'd done . . . not that there was a God . . . or was there?

As the weeks passed, Richard began to get better. Eventually he was able to leave the sanatorium but he still needed to be somewhere quiet where he could rest. He decided to go to a little mountain village, and there he met a man who would help to change the course of his life.

Christian Wolfkes was the village carpenter. He was old and sick but he had one ambition to fulfil before he died: he wanted to help a Jewish person to know Jesus. The trouble was, there were no Jews living in his village. He'd been asking God to do something about it for a long time! Now God had answered his prayer.

Richard began to read the Bible which the carpenter lent him. He was amazed at the things Jesus said and did. He read how Jesus suffered and he knew that his followers often had to suffer, too. Richard didn't want that but then he knew that Jesus was telling him not to be afraid. As he thought about the mess his life was in, Richard decided he must ask Jesus to be his friend. And he realised that Jesus was God, the God he'd said did not exist. How wrong he'd been!

'Richard, how could you!' Sabina was horrified that her husband had become a Christian. She knew that so-called Christians had done terrible things to Jews in the past. As a little girl, she had been taught to look the other way when she passed a Christian church. Besides, she wanted to enjoy life. She didn't want to bother about pleasing God.

One night Richard and Sabina were at a party, but Sabina found she was not enjoying herself. People were getting drunk. The room was filled with cigarette smoke. Sabina knew that her idea of having a good time had been wrong. By the time they left, Sabina had made up her mind that she, too, wanted to be a follower of Jesus.

The Wurmbrands stayed away from wild parties now. They would have liked to settle down and live in peace. They certainly didn't go looking for trouble, but it seemed that following Jesus brought trouble to them. Many of their Jewish friends turned against them, but Richard was not put off. He longed to help others, Jews and non-Jews, to become Christians. He was delighted when he was offered a job in Bucharest with a society calling itself the Anglican Mission to Jews.

Sabina's baby boy, Mihai, was born in 1939. It was to be a terrible year for the people of Rumania, especially the Jews. Their country was caught between the Russian Communists to the north and the German Nazis to the west. Both groups were against the Jews. Then in 1940, the Iron Guard, hard, cruel men, who had been trained by the Nazis, began a campaign of terror against the Jews in Rumania.

Many, many frightened people needed help.

'Where can we go?' they wondered. 'Try the Wurm-brands' flat,' came the reply. Richard and Sabina never turned anyone away: Christians, Jews, gypsies, all found a refuge and Sabina often had to water down the soup to make enough for everyone.

At the end of 1940, German troops occupied Rumania. When Richard spoke out against the Nazis and the terrible things they were doing, he knew that he might end up in prison – and he *did* on several occasions. He didn't know then that even harder things would happen to him after the Nazis had been defeated.

In 1944, Russian troops invaded Rumania and most of the people were glad to see them! Soon they would be freed from the hated Nazis. As the columns of Soviet tanks approached Bucharest, Richard had an idea.

'Let's go and meet the soldiers, Sabina,' he said. 'They have been taught that God is not there, but we know that he is! We could give some Russian Bibles as presents.'

They succeeded in giving some Bibles away, but the Communist sergeant was not impressed. They would have to change their tactics!

A day later, Richard and his five year old son were out in the town. Two Russian soldiers, a man and a woman, were having problems in a shop and they didn't speak Russian.

'Can I help you?' asked Richard, speaking in Rus-sian. He acted as an interpreter for them and helped them to buy what they wanted. Then the Russian woman asked, 'Could you tell me which are the best shops for women's clothes?' Richard thought quickly. If the couple would come to his home, perhaps they could talk about more important things than clothes? And so he invited them for lunch to meet his wife. Sabina would show the Russian lady the shops in the afternoon. But they didn't get back to the shops that day. They were too busy discussing a man called Jesus!

The Wurmbrands' home was still open house to all in need, but now it was German soldiers on the run and Rumanians who had sided with the Nazis who needed help. Richard and Sabina hated the cruel things the Nazis had done, but they knew that Jesus wanted them to love their enemies as well as their friends. And so they were willing to hide the despised and desperate Nazis. By a miracle, these people never arrived at the Wurmbrands' home at the same time as the Russian soldiers whom Sabina and Richard also entertained!

One of the Wurmbrands' Russian friends was Ivan. He arrived, with some other soldiers, on their doorstep one day selling umbrellas. Richard didn't want to buy one of the umbrellas, which he knew were probably stolen, but he asked the soldiers to come in. Then Sabina and Ivan recognised each other. She had given him a Bible when he first entered Bucharest. Some time later, after many hours discussing the Bible with Richard, the young Russian sergeant became a Christian.

The war ended and everyone hoped for happier times. But in Rumania, the Communists took over the government.

'We have to go to a special meeting of Christian leaders,' Richard told Sabina. 'The speeches will be on the radio, so everyone in Rumania will know what is said.'

There were four thousand people packed into the hall. The Wurmbrands became more and more unhappy as they listened to the speeches. Men were saying that there was really no difference between Communism and Christianity. At last, Sabina could bear it no longer. She wanted Richard to stand up and say something. You could have heard a pin drop as Richard reached the microphone on the stage.

'We should be bringing glory to God, not siding with people who say he does not even exist,' Richard told his audience. The Communists began to look uneasy, but many of the Christian leaders started to clap. They were glad that someone had the courage to say what they really believed. The cable to the microphone was cut, but not before Richard's message had been broadcast all over Rumania.

There were still many Russian soldiers in the country. One of their 'hobbies' was collecting (often stealing) watches which they would then sell back to the Rumanians. This gave Richard an idea.

'If we went to the barracks and pretended to be buying watches, we could then tell some of the soldiers about Jesus,' he thought. It was a risky business, but it worked! One of the soldiers who wanted to hear the stories of Jesus would stand behind Richard. If he spotted someone who would not approve, he squeezed Richard's shoulder. Then Richard would start to talk about the watches instead.

Richard and his friends had to do their work secretly. They were called the Underground Church and they knew they were always in danger of being put into prison. When the Secret Police came to arrest Richard, they were amazed at how calm he seemed. After singing a hymn, praying and reading the Bible he went with them without a struggle.

Six weeks later, Richard was out of prison but he was still in great danger. It was not safe for him to be in Rumania.

'Why don't you get out while you can?' said his friends.

'Perhaps it would be best,' thought Richard. 'How can I help the church if I'm in prison?' But one day, Sabina and Richard were meeting secretly with some other Christians, when one of them had a special message from God. Richard knew that the message was for him. He must not leave Rumania. God wanted him to stay.

Not long after, Richard was walking to church alone through the snowy streets of Bucharest. He wanted to get to church early this Sunday morning as he had some things to get ready for a wedding service in the afternoon. Suddenly, a big black car came up behind him and screeched to a halt. Seconds later, Richard was being bundled into the car. No one saw it happen. No one could tell Sabina what had happened to her husband. And she wouldn't see him again for a *very* long time.

Richard sat on his wooden bed and stared round his cell. He couldn't see through the window near the ceiling and the dirty glass hardly let in any light. 'How long before they begin to ask questions?' he wondered. He knew so much that the Secret Police would also like to know. Would he crack up under torture? Whatever happened, he didn't want to betray the others in the Underground Church.

Sabina was getting more and more worried. She phoned several hospitals to see if Richard had been in an accident. She tried the prisons – but none of them admitted to having Pastor Wurmbrand as a prisoner. It was many weeks later before she received a message from Richard smuggled out of prison by one of the warders. It was only a few words, but she knew it was Richard's writing.

'He's still alive,' she sighed. 'And he says he is well.'

Inside the prison, the Secret Police were stepping up the pressure on Richard. For nights he was not allowed to sleep. He was beaten and hurt in other ways.

'Names! We want names!' his interrogator told him. At last Richard took the paper and wrote a list. It took them several days to discover that everyone on Richard's list had either left the country or was dead!

Richard's captors decided on a new tactic. He was moved to solitary confinement. From his cell under the ground he could hear – nothing. Would the silence and boredom drive him mad? Richard could still talk to God and he knew God was there with him. He saved a few crumbs from his ration of bread to mix with flakes of paint from the wall and made knights and castles and pawns so that he could play chess against himself.

'Tap, tap, tap.' Richard was on his bed when he heard the sound. It was the prisoner in the cell next to his! Gradually they began to 'talk' to each other by tapping in code. More and more prisoners joined in. Richard was even able to tap out his message of the love of Jesus.

'We know what you are up to!' Lieutenant Grecu, the interrogator, said. The guards had discovered what was happening. Grecu wanted to know more. Richard told him he was a follower of Jesus who had taught him to love his enemies. Grecu was intrigued. Instead of punishing Richard, he asked him to tell him more about God. Soon after, Lieutenant Grecu disappeared. Perhaps he, too, was now a prisoner.

Richard's cough was back again. Eventually his TB was so bad that he was moved to a prison hospital. He was put in Room 4 with several other very sick patients. No one had ever left Room 4 alive, and no warders dared to go in the room in case they caught TB.

In spite of their suffering, the patients generally got on well together. They told jokes to cheer each other up. And Richard was able to help many to be at peace with God before they died.

One day a new prisoner arrived in Room 4. He had TB of the spine and so he had to wear a plaster cast round his body. Richard's eyes grew wide as the man fumbled in the top of his cast and produced a book. It wasn't just any old book, it was part of the Bible, John's Gospel. The book gave new hope to Richard and the other prisoners. And before long, they had some more good news.

'The Commandant in charge of the prison has been sacked,' went the rumour. Sure enough, it was true and conditions for the prisoners got slightly better. Richard grew strong enough to get out of bed. The doctor was amazed that he had survived. Richard left the dreaded Room 4 – still alive!

Richard needed all his new strength to cope with some shattering news passed on by a friend. Sabina had also been arrested and sent to work as a slave labourer. Richard could hardly bear to think about it.

'What happened to Mihai?' he wondered. 'How long was Sabina away?' At least the friend had told him that Sabina was still alive.

'There's a letter for you.' Richard could hardly believe it. It was the first letter he'd received during his time in prison – and it was from Sabina. What's more, she told him that he would soon be having a visit from Mihai, the son he had not seen for seven years.

They were not allowed to talk for long and the guards were listening. But Richard was thrilled to see Mihai, a tall young man of sixteen, and to know that he was still a follower of Jesus.

For the next year, Richard was moved from one prison to another, suffering terribly. Then one day he was called for interrogation again. But once outside his cell, a man handed him an official looking paper. There had been an amnesty. He was free!

Looking like a scarecrow, Richard began to walk down the road from the prison. The local people guessed where he'd come from. Someone gave him money to take the tram into Bucharest. Soon he was at his own front door and then he was hugging Sabina, as tears rolled down his cheeks.

Eight years in prison had changed Richard from a tall, handsome man into a grey-faced 'skeleton', but they had not broken his spirit. He was determined to continue preaching, in spite of the dangers. He was not surprised when, less than three years after his release, he was once again arrested by the Secret Police.

For five years Richard suffered more cruelty and hardship in prison. He was forced to listen to tapes for hours on end telling him that Christianity was stupid, that Communism was good, that he should give up his faith. But he didn't give up. God helped him even to pray for those who tortured him.

In June, 1964 the prisoners were ordered to assemble in a big hall in the prison.

'What's happening?' everyone wondered. The prison Commandant had something important to say. Richard's heart leapt as he took it in. Another amnesty! Political prisoners would be freed! He would soon breathe fresh air again.

Six months later, two British Christians visited Rumania. Richard met them in church and invited them to his home. Warily, they climbed the stairs to the attic room where Richard, Sabina and Mihai were living. Then they listened in amazement as Richard told his story. They knew they must do what they could to help. And so it was that the Wurmbrands were finally put on a plane to leave Rumania. Christians from other countries had paid the Rumanian government to let them go.

As he flew to freedom, Richard knew that his work was far from over. He must do all he could to tell people about the suffering Christians in Communist countries: men and women like himself, whose only crime was to follow Jesus.

Since leaving Rumania, Richard Wurmbrand has travelled the world spreading his message and

Christian Missions to the Communist World have been started in forty-three different countries.

Have you read these other Tiger books?

The King's Quest
Lynette Bishop

It began one ordinary day at breakfast. Simon and Jenny had just welcomed the visitor who was to share their holiday when news of the invasion stunned them. The Grey Gunners from the planet Gehalla had landed. But the visitor had brought a mysterious message and an exciting mission for Simon and Jenny with consequences for this planet and beyond.

Dothan the Dreamer
Nora Rock

Dothan daydreams a lot. After all, herding goats is not very exciting. Then Elijah, the man of God, comes to stay at Dothan's house and strange things begin to happen. Life changes for Dothan and some of his dreams begin to come true. He gets to visit the city of Tyre and discovers that he can draw and carve as well as some of the craftsmen there. But how can he, a poor country boy, find the money to train as a silversmith? God has ways for us all, he discovers.